"J
JOY...in the Lord
Y   always *

dear * David and * Mary

Molly + Irene Bronner
and FAMILY
and TEAM

* CHRISTMAS *
* 2007

PICTURESQUE STORY of

BRONNER'S CHRISTmas WONDERLAND
Frankenmuth, Mich.
®

as related by

Wally Bronner

Originator

Published by

BRONNER'S CHRISTmas WONDERLAND

25 Christmas Lane

Frankenmuth, Michigan 48734-0176

USA

www.bronners.com

PICTURESQUE STORY of BRONNER'S CHRISTmas WONDERLAND

Published by
BRONNER'S CHRISTmas WONDERLAND
25 Christmas Lane
Frankenmuth, Michigan 48734-0176

On the internet, visit www.bronners.com

ISBN - 0-9755061-2-9
Library of Congress Control Number: 2005908503

First Edition

Printed in the USA
Sheridan Books, Inc. - Ann Arbor, Michigan

Table of Contents

Dedicated to
God

FROM WHOM ALL BLESSINGS FLOW

"God gives to all some talent,
Some special work to do.
Should we not use these talents,
Though they be just a few?
If we but look around us,
We'll see jobs by the score.
So, use that little talent,
And God will give you more."

by
Elfrieda Almandinger Frueh

 *...in the Lord*
...always

3

Dedicated to

MILLIONS AND MILLIONS OF

PAST, PRESENT AND FUTURE *Guests*

and many more

Dedicated to

THOUSANDS OF INNOVATIVE AND LOYAL

Suppliers

Alpenländische Christbaumschmuckfabrik

Fontanini

Lauscha Glas Creation

THEWALT GMBH

soffieria de carlini SINCE 1947

MATTHÄI

ENESCO GROUP, INC.

FRIEDEL

Friedrich Seiler GmbH

Goebel M.J. Hummel

BARCANA INC.

Christian ULBRICHT Handcrafted in Germany since 1928

Moranduzzo

ORNEX LTD.
CZECH REPUBLIC JABLONEC NAD NISOU

Roman, Inc.

MIDWEST OF CANNON FALLS

CARPENTER DECORATING

GP Designs LLC

NOMA

JABLONEX

Seraphim Classics
Heaven on Earth

DICKSONS

caffco

Erwin Eichhorn

SANTA'S HOLIDAYS ARE WORLD
KURT S. ADLER
SINCE 1946

BARTHELMESS U.S.A.

Christmas by Krebs

THE LEGACY NOVELTY CO., LTD.

Merck Family's
Old World Christmas

Sterling

Manufacturers of Quality Animated Displays
HAMBERGER Displays

STEINBACH GMBH

PRECIOUS MOMENTS COMPANY

also... Glass artisans
from Poland and Romania

and many more

Dedicated to
LOCAL, STATE, NATIONAL & INTERNATIONAL
Media

Newspapers

Adirondack Daily Enterprise ✦ Angola Herald-Republican ✦ Arizona Republic Bay City Times ✦ Benton Harbor-St. Joseph Herald-Palladium ✦ Buffalo News ✦ Chicago Sun-Times ✦ Clare County Review Columbus Dispatch ✦ Corpus Christi Caller-Times ✦ Dallas Morning News ✦ Detroit Free Press ✦ Detroit News ✦ Elkhart Truth Elmira Star-Gazette ✦ Falfurrias Facts Findlay Courier ✦ Flint Journal ✦ Fort Worth Star-Telegram ✦ Frankenmuth News Frankfurter Allgemeine ✦ Frankfurter Zeitung Gautier Independent ✦ Grand Rapids Press Hamilton Spectator ✦ Jackson Citizen Patriot Kiplingers ✦ Lansing State Journal ✦ Louisville Courier-Journal ✦ Mid-Michigan Winter Traveler ✦ Miami Herald ✦ Munster Times Napoleon Northwest Signal ✦ Oakland Press Polish Weekly ✦ Saginaw News ✦ Saginaw Township Times ✦ Salzburger Nachrichten Sebewaing Newsweekly ✦ Sebring News-Sun South Bend Tribune ✦ Toledo Blade Toronto Star ✦ Tuscola County Advertiser USA Today ✦ Wall Street Journal ✦ Washington Post ✦ West Michigan Senior Times

Radio

WCTC ✦ WDRQ ✦ WGDN WGN✦WHNN ✦ WIOG ✦ WJIM ✦ WJR WKCQ ✦ WKNX ✦ WLJN ✦ WMUZ WSAM ✦ WSGW ✦ WSNL ✦ WTRN WUFL ✦ WUGN ✦ WWJ Cape Talk Radio, South Africa The Handyman Show with Glenn Haege Lutheran Hour Ministries Travel & Adventure with Michael Dwyer

Television

ABC	WAQP
BBC	WEYI
CBN	WJRT
CBS	WKBD
CNN	WLNS
MDR	WNDU
FOX	WNEM
NBC	WOOD
ORF	WOTV
PBS	WREX
RB	WSMH
ZDF	WTVG
WWUP	WWJ TV 62
WZZM	WWTV
UPN 50	

Charter Communications
Comcast Cable
Food Network
Get Connected TV
HGTV
Lutheran Ministries Media
TCT Ministries
Big Breakfast
CBS Sunday Morning
Carol Duvall Show
Good Morning Britain
Movin' On with Jim & Ron
Northern Experience
On Main Street
Today Show

Magazines

AAA Home & Away ✦ Air Conditioning, Heating, & Refrigeration News ✦ All You American Christmas Tree Journal American Profile ✦ Angels on Earth Association Spotlight ✦ Attaché ✦ Better Homes and Gardens ✦ Business Advocate ✦ Bus Tours Magazine ✦ Celebrate 365 ✦ Christian Retailing Christian Life ✦ CITY Parent ✦ Coast to Coast Collector Editions ✦ Collector's Mart Commercial Christmas Décor ✦ Coronet Creche Herald ✦ Country Sampler Decorating Ideas ✦ Destinations ✦ Dance Spirit Dance Teacher ✦ Enesco Seasons Magazine Festival ✦ Fifty-Six ✦ Floral Management Ford Times ✦ Gifts and Decorative Accessories Giftware Business ✦ Giftware News ✦ Going Places ✦ Good Housekeeping ✦ Good Sam Club Magazine ✦ Grit ✦ Group Tour Magazine Happiness ✦ Leading Edge ✦ Leisure Group Travel ✦ Log Home Design Ideas ✦ Log Home Living ✦ Mary Beth's Christmas Ornament Special ✦ Mary Beth's Beanies & More Michigan Bell ✦ Michigan Living ✦ Michigan Magazine ✦ Michigan Meetings & Events Midwest Living ✦ Michigan Lutheran Michigan Travel Ideas ✦ Michigan Tourist Monthly ✦ Mi Gente Magazine ✦ Museums & More ✦ National Geographic Traveler Nation's Business ✦ Noise ✦ Orange County Home ✦ Packaged Travel Insider ✦ People Magazine ✦ Postcard Collector ✦ Salvation Army War Cry ✦ Selling Christmas Decorations Southern Accents ✦ Specialty Retail Report Standard Torch ✦ Tampa Bay Magazine Today's Business ✦ Today's Christian ✦ Traffic World Magazine ✦ Trailer Life ✦ Travel America USA Weekend ✦ Woman's Day Best Ideas for Christmas ✦ X.O.P. International

THE MEDIA HAS BEEN VERY GENEROUS IN TELLING THE PICTURESQUE STORY OF BRONNER'S

and many more

Dedicated to Loyal Staff

Over 3,500 have served on the team since 1945

During peak season there are over 500 on the team

2005 BRONNER MANAGERS: (seated) Linda McInerney, Dennis Pfund, Lanny Nuechterlein, Michael Laux, Sandra Schafsnitz (standing) Joanne Brewer, Betty Caswell, Cindy Baxter, Scott Miller, Anne Koehler, Wahnita Schiefer

The Bronner family is very thankful to God for the pleasing blend of talents that comprise the many departments...

Store personnel	Santa	Commercial
Customer Service	Ornament Personalizing	Office
Sparkle	Catalog and Internet	Buyers
Season's Eatings Snack Area	Receiving	Human Resources
Decorating and Design	Maintenance	Supervisors
Visual Merchandising	Wholesale & Custom Ornaments	Managers
Web Merchandising		Shipping

11

Dedicated to the Entire Family

Front row: Maria Bronner Sutorik, Carla Bronner Spletzer, Wally Bronner, Irene Bronner, Greg Spletzer, Wayne Bronner
Back row: Christopher Sutorik, Bob Spletzer, Ryan Spletzer, Paul Spletzer, Dietrich Bronner, Lorene Scholtz Bronner, Garrett Bronner, Randy Bronner

Parents Herman and Ella

Brother Arnold

Sister Helen

Aunt Hattie Hubinger

13

Acknowledgements

DORIS PAUL of Lansing, Michigan, is credited for authoring the first booklet (1981) on the Bronner business. Some segments of her writings are included in this book.

JEANNE BRAEUTIGAM joined the Bronner team in 1963. She has kept excellent files of the thousands of slides and "zillions" of photos that Wally snapped over the years. Her expertise helped the compilation of this book's contents.

PRODUCTION TEAM

The research, editorial and graphic skills of our **OFFICE STAFF** and **BRONNER FAMILY MEMBERS** were contributors in the production of this book. **LORI LIBKA** edited the text, **LISA KRAUSE** did the layout, and the others assisted with the research.

Lori Libka, Jen Harden, Ellen Mocny, Sue Kern, Joanne Brewer, Lisa Krause, Karen Hoffman, Jeanne Braeutigam

1 Introduction

Since "a picture is worth a thousand words," it is hoped that for every 1,000 words in this condensed story, the reader will "picture" a segment of history.

A series of books could be written about the details of various phases of the Bronner business. The goal of this publication, however, is to present a brief, pertinent history.

BRONNER'S CHRISTmas WONDERLAND, located in the picturesque, mid-Michigan town of Frankenmuth, is a thriving business through which its owners, Wallace (Wally) & Irene Bronner and family, strive to promote the spirit expressed in the familiar carol, "Joy to the world! The Lord is come!" To keep that spirit alive throughout the year, doors are open 361 days of the year.

Nestled on 27 acres of uniquely landscaped grounds (part of a 45-acre tract), Bronner's Alpine-design building spans 7.35 acres (5.5 football fields) and features a shopping wonderland of ornaments, decorations, and gifts for every season, reason and budget. Each year, more than two million guests from around the world come to Frankenmuth to wander through this Christmas wonderland. As one of Michigan's most visited tourist attractions, Bronner's is recognized by AAA and other automobile associations in the North American continent.

Guests of all ages - from babes-in-arms and wide-eyed children to adults that are still children at heart - are excited by the dazzling displays at BRONNER'S CHRISTmas WONDERLAND. Motorcoach tours and groups from many states, provinces, and nations visit Bronner's annually.

The single pointer on the clock dial at the entrance to BRONNER'S CHRISTmas WONDERLAND indicates the time of year: half-past July, a quarter till November, or "straight-up" December. No matter what the time or season may be, guests are swept along by the feeling of Christmas from the moment they enter.

It has been estimated that a leisurely "walk-through" takes about two hours. However, for many people a longer time is desired. There is so much to see. Bronner's is a shopper's dream, especially for Christmas lovers! Some have named the experience "shopper-tainment."

The balconies, which surround a large portion of the salesroom, afford space for displays that delight the eye. Industrious elves help Santa in his workshop. Mufflered carolers sing their hearts out.

One area is devoted to Nativity scenes, with angels heralding the good news through their long, golden trumpets. The store features more than 500 beautiful Nativity scenes from many nations around the world, including Bronner's exclusive, life-size Nativity.

Visiting and revisiting the wonderland has become a tradition for many people of all ages. First-time and repeat guests that visit numerous times a year are equally thrilled with the seemingly ever-changing variety of trims and gifts ... the spirit of CHRISTmas is ever present at Bronner's in Frankenmuth, Michigan.

The Bronner family emphasizes the religious aspect of the holiday season, stocking Bibles in numerous languages. Hanging above a beautiful, life-size manger scene is a picture of Jesus knocking at the door of the United Nations Building (entitled "Prince of Peace"). It is a visual reference to Biblical words from Revelations 3:20, "Behold I stand at the door and knock; if anyone hears my voice and opens the door, I will come in." (Coincidentally, Revelations 3:20 happens to be Wally's confirmation text.)

"The angels announced, 'Peace on earth, good will to men,' to the shepherds on the eve of Christ's birth. Jesus Christ himself is that Prince of Peace and the only hope for a troubled world. It is in this frame of mind that guests are welcomed to BRONNER'S CHRISTmas WONDERLAND," says Irene Bronner.

To help carry this message, it is the custom of Bronner's to include a religious tract with every package and piece of mail.

The philosophy underlying the business is that the Christmas season is an especially joyful time of the year. Bronner's goal is to provide a worldwide selection of decorations and gifts for a birthday observance - the birthday of Christ the Savior. The business was built on the idea of celebrating the significance of the Christ Child's birth daily - not just limiting it to the traditional twelve days of Christmas. Therefore, Bronner's motto is:

Enjoy CHRISTmas, It's HIS Birthday;

Enjoy LIFE, It's HIS Way.

THANK GOD FOR THE ARMED FORCES - Throughout the years of our business, many of our team have served in the military to protect our nation's freedoms. With an attitude of gratitude, we remember the dedication of everyone on our team and others in our nation who have served, including those who made the supreme sacrifice. The precious freedoms are speech, press, the rights to assemble and petition government, and the free exercise of religion.

"Joy to the World the Lord is Come"

THE BUSINESS NAME APPEARS IN AN ORNAMENT-SHAPED LOGO accented with a sprig of greenery. The cross-shaped star and capitalized "CHRIST" with lowercase "mas" emphasize the reason for the season of Christmas. (Designed by Wally).

OPEN 361 DAYS

BRONNER'S CHRISTmas WONDERLAND
Frankenmuth, Mich.
®

WORLD'S LARGEST CHRISTMAS STORE

THE FLOOR AREA of Bronner's Alpine-design building **IS THE SIZE OF 5.5 FOOTBALL FIELDS**. The building and landscaping occupy 27 acres of a 45-acre tract. Parking lots accommodate 1,250 cars and 50 motorcoaches.

The **Bronner Motto**

The Bible quotation Revelation 3:20 is Wally's confirmation text. The painting, **"PRINCE OF PEACE"** by Harry Anderson, is meaningful to Wally and hangs in the entrance as a welcome to all who enter.

> Behold, I stand at the door and knock: If anyone hears my voice and opens the door, I will come in ...
> REVELATION 3:20

"ENJOY CHRISTmas, IT'S HIS BIRTHDAY; ENJOY LIFE, IT'S HIS WAY" is the motto for the business started by originator Wally Bronner and his wife Irene.

At Bronner's, it's Christmas 12 months a year as indicated by the unique clock.

Bronner's adapted its motto from a Christmas card that **REV. ELMER WITT**, his wife Virginia, and their family sent to the Bronners. **VIRGINIA AUTHORED THE CARD'S TEXT.**

21

The Bronner-produced, life-sized, fiberglass **NATIVITY SCENE AND HERALDING ANGEL** in front of the south and west entrances are favorite photo spots.

The store is a **POPULAR DESTINATION** for a multitude of motorcoach travelers from Canada and the USA.

The 2002 addition continues the **ALPINE THEME**.

A Christmas Wonderland

The spacious store features 50,000 trims and gifts from around the world.

The array of over **500 NATIVITY SCENES**, ranging in size from miniature to life-size, is popular year round for gifts and displays.

Irene Bronner accepts the 1976 **EMBASSY OF MICHIGAN TOURISM AWARD** presented to the Bronners by Governor William Milliken.

23

"WALLY - YOU SHOULD WRITE A BOOK" Such were the comments from various people and especially Walter John Ernst Rummel from Sebewaing, Michigan. He is an author and newspaper editor. When Walt said, "You know, none of us are getting any younger," I made the decision God-willing to author four books by midnight of March 8, 2007, before I attain the 80 plateau on March 9.

The themes for the books are:

1. Picturesque History of Bronner's CHRISTmas Wonderland

2. Sharing Christmas JOY 365 Days a Year

3. Reflections, Quips, Quotes, Phrases and Speech Excerpts

4. CHRISTmas Comments and Wonders

EARNING ORDERS AND REORDERS - When Wally was a novice sign painter, he made a visit to the office of James Wickson, president of Frankenmuth's Universal Engineering, and told Mr. Wickson that he would like the chance to hand letter Universal's company vehicles. Mr. Wickson thanked Wally for the visit and said that he would keep him in mind. Mr. Wickson explained that those currently lettering his vehicles were doing satisfactory work and deserved his continued business. That taught Wally to wait patiently for the prospective buyer to accept the offer of the seller and to do only the best work to earn reorders and new clients. Many orders and reorders eventually followed from Mr. Wickson and his staff.

2 | Wally Bronner's Frankenmuth Heritage

Wallace Bronner's grandfather, Johann Bronner, was born in Pfaffenhofen, Germany, near Heilbronn, on May 29, 1857. He boarded a ship for America in 1882 at the age of 25; upon his arrival in America, he settled in Frankenmuth, Michigan, a "mission colony" that had been established in 1845 by a group of German Lutherans whose goal was to bring the gospel to Native Americans and others in the area.

Johann worked in stone and brick masonry, a family trade he had learned from his father in Germany. On July 21, 1889, he married Maria Barbara Rohn. They had seven children in all - the third-born child was Herman, Wally's father. Herman continued in his father's masonry trade and later constructed the first permanent building for BRONNER'S CHRISTmas WONDERLAND at 121 E. Tuscola Street in Frankenmuth.

Wally's mother Ella was the second oldest child of Gottfried and Maria Hubinger. Gottfried's father, Johann Matthias Hubinger, arrived in the USA in 1846 as a member of the second group of Frankenmuth's settlers. The Hubinger family had a farm, orchard, and a general grocery store that also housed the post office and the bank. Gottfried was president of the Village of Frankenmuth from March 12, 1917, to January 3, 1928.

Ella's grandfather was Simon Riedel, who came to St. Lorenz Church in Frankenmuth from Eden, New York, in 1854. (He had come to New York state from Germany sometime between 1848 and 1851.) Simon was the first full-time church musician and teacher for the St. Lorenz Christian Day School, which served the pioneer group of German Lutheran settlers in Frankenmuth.

The Christian principles, trades, and professions of Wally's ancestors truly influenced his vocational choices.

Origin of Frankenmuth

FRANKENMUTH WAS FOUNDED IN 1845 by fifteen settlers from Neuendettelsau, Germany. One half of the log cabin was used as the church and school; the other half was the dwelling for the pastor and his wife. William "Tiny" Zehnder and his wife Dorothy donated the pictured replica in 1962.

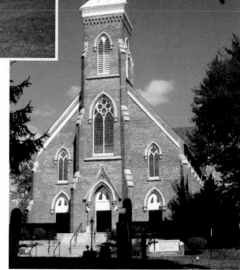

In 1880, a brick church was erected. It was enlarged in 1967, to seat 1,200.

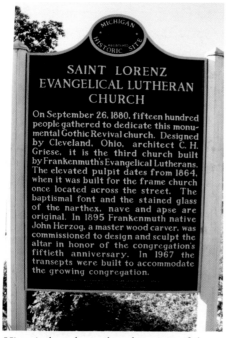

Historical markers relate the origin of the St. Lorenz Lutheran Church and Frankenmuth.

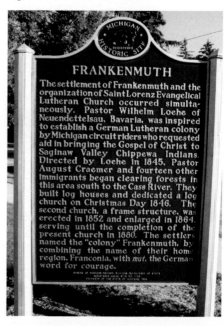

SAINT LORENZ EVANGELICAL LUTHERAN CHURCH

On September 26, 1880, fifteen hundred people gathered to dedicate this monumental Gothic Revival church. Designed by Cleveland, Ohio, architect C. H. Griese, it is the third church built by Frankenmuth's Evangelical Lutherans. The elevated pulpit dates from 1864, when it was built for the frame church once located across the street. The baptismal font and the stained glass of the narthex, nave and apse are original. In 1895 Frankenmuth native John Herzog, a master wood carver, was commissioned to design and sculpt the altar in honor of the congregation's fiftieth anniversary. In 1967 the transepts were built to accommodate the growing congregation.

FRANKENMUTH

The settlement of Frankenmuth and the organization of Saint Lorenz Evangelical Lutheran Church occurred simultaneously. Pastor Wilhelm Loehe of Neuendettelsau, Bavaria, was inspired to establish a German Lutheran colony by Michigan circuit riders who requested aid in bringing the Gospel of Christ to Saginaw Valley Chippewa Indians. Directed by Loehe in 1845, Pastor August Craemer and fourteen other immigrants began clearing forests in this area south to the Cass River. They built log houses and dedicated a log church on Christmas Day 1846. The second church, a frame structure, was erected in 1852 and enlarged in 1864, serving until the completion of the present church in 1880. The settlers named the "colony" Frankenmuth, by combining the name of their home region, Franconia, with *mut*, the German word for courage.

Ancestry

WALLY'S PARENTS ELLA and **HERMAN BRONNER**, older brother Arnold and sister Helen (1937 family photo). Wally's father Herman and his brothers followed the building trade.

GRANDPARENTS ON FATHER'S SIDE, Johann and Maria (Rohn) Bronner. Johann, a stone mason and builder by trade, came to America in 1882.

GRANDPARENTS ON MOTHER'S SIDE, Gottfried and Maria (Riedel) Hubinger. The Hubingers operated a general store and farm.

GREAT-GRANDFATHER Simon Riedel was the first full-time church musician and teacher at St. Lorenz.

Early Days

Hubinger General Store, late 1800s.

WALLY WAS INTRODUCED TO THE RETAIL BUSINESS by Grandpa Gottfried Hubinger (above photo) and Wally's Aunt "Hattie" Hedwig Hubinger (right photo).

In 1903, lightning started a fire that burned the original wooden store to the ground.
A new building of brick was constructed that same year.

28

Artistry

Wally's mother encouraged him to help with Christmas decorations. The framed Nativity scene above the mantel, one of **WALLY'S FIRST CHRISTMAS DECORATIONS**, is now on display in Bronner's program center.

Wally's father constructed the **FAMILY HOME** in 1928 at the northwest corner of Haas and East Tuscola Streets. Wally first dabbled in hand-crafted and hand-lettered signs and Christmas decorations in the basement of this home.

The intricate brick designs over the windows were father Herman's building trademark.

Wally's father was the contractor for the Frankenmuth Bank building on the northeast corner of Main and Tuscola Streets.

Herman's father Johann was a stonecutter and constructed unique foundations, chimneys, and columns.

29

FRANKENMUTH'S QUEST FOR A CREST - In 1962 the city council appointed Wally and three other committee members to design a crest for the city. The city adapted the official shield in 1963. **Frankenmuth means "courage of the Franconians."** German settlers arrived in Frankenmuth in 1845 to live and teach Christianity among the Indians.

Eagle - Americanism	Muth - Courage
Grain - First Settlers	Diamonds - Bavaria
Franken - Ancestral Homeland	Luther's Seal - Christianity

HOBBY BECOMES A BUSINESS - Dr. Kirchgeorg advised Wally to "keep searching for a vocation that provides joy - where one may tire of long hours but never of the type of work." That thought made Wally realize his art hobby could become a business that would serve the needs of many. Wally has enjoyed his hobby for over 60 years.

FRANKENMUTH IS FAMOUS FOR FOOD - That's a slogan used by Wally during some speeches. The complete message is Frankenmuth is famous for food...

Food for the eye...the beauty of the community.

Food for the palate...the good cooking by citizens and chefs.

Food for the soul...the spiritual encouragement from Frankenmuth's fine churches and the Silent Night Memorial Chapel.

3 | Origin of the Business

During a period of nearly six decades, BRONNER'S CHRISTmas WONDERLAND developed from the humblest beginning to the world's largest Christmas store. It supplies Christmas and all-season decorations for homes, churches, businesses, industries, cities, streets, parks, malls, shopping centers, movie studios, parades, and parties. Bronner's also supplies other retailers and catalog firms.

Contributing to the joy of Christmas throughout the nation and the world, Bronner's ships merchandise to every state and territory in the union, to every province in Canada, and to numerous nations. Bronner's first major export shipment of ornaments, Nativity sets, and decorations was sent to Myer's Emporium in Australia in 1979. Bronner's life-size fiberglass Nativity set has been shipped to five continents. After the Berlin Wall came down, the Wohlfart family of Rothenburg on the Tauber purchased a life-size Nativity for display in the city center of Leipzig, Germany. In 1993, a similar set was supplied for the Berlin Christmas Market near Memorial Church.

In addition to the mammoth display in Frankenmuth, Michigan, a portion of Bronner's decorations and Nativity scenes are available through Bronner's catalog and via online shopping at www.bronners.com.

Many people who visit the immense display ask how such a business developed and who was responsible. Originator Wallace Bronner started as a sign painter. It all began in 1943 in the basement of 290 Haas Street in Frankenmuth, the home of his parents, Herman and Ella Bronner, when Wally was sixteen years old. His artistic nature was first expressed while framing a paper Nativity scene for his parents when he was only twelve. This piece and his first watercolor, a winter scene entered in an art show sponsored by Leonard Zehnder of the Zehnder family at Zehnder's Restaurant in the late '40s, are now displayed in the program center at BRONNER'S CHRISTmas WONDERLAND.

During the early years when Wally was beginning what was to become a successful career in sign painting, he also worked part-time in his Aunt Hattie Hubinger's grocery store, clerking and decorating the display windows. After graduation from high school in 1945, Wally attended the Saginaw Business Institute (currently Davenport University) for two years, acquiring skills that proved helpful in developing his own business in later years.

His signs and displays in his aunt's grocery windows attracted the attention of other businesses and industries. Before long, they asked the young artist to prepare displays and signs for them. ("Signtists" and "signologists" were the catchwords that sign painters used to describe their craft.) From the beginning, the business established by the young sign painter was officially named Bronner Display and Sign Advertising. The date (1945) also marked the centennial year for Frankenmuth (settled one hundred years previously by German colonists including missionaries to the Native Americans). It was a happy coincidence that led Wally to many jobs decorating store windows and parade floats, and painting signs – all in celebration of the centennial. William Mossner was among the first farmers to order a barn sign from Bronner's Display and Signs in the late 1940s.

In 1946 business expanded at a rapid rate. The first truck doors lettered by the sign business were ordered by Emil Zuellig for Paul Zuellig & Son, the Birch Run coal business Emil ran with his father Paul.

The freelance window-display business in the four-county area increased as did the decorating of fair booths. In order to handle the multitude of requests, Wally called on his brother Arnold and sister Helen Bronner Rupprecht to assist him occasionally on a part-time basis. During this busy year (1947) he also hired other part-time help. Roland Gugel assisted in painting sign panels.

The original Roth Carpentry Shop (behind Hubinger's Grocery), served as Wally's sign-painting shop during the warm months. Display props and decorations were stored in the second story of the grocery store.

When the infant display and sign business grew to the point that Wally could not handle it alone, he hired his first part-time salesman, Waldo Vanek, in 1948. Mr. Vanek's main assignment was to call on area farmers to solicit name signs for their barns. In 1949 Wally hired a high school student, Edward Beyerlein, to assist him part-time. Eddie eventually became the first full-time staff member for Bronner Display and Sign Advertising. (He retired in 1994 after 46 years with the business. In his retirement, Eddie and his wife Jane handcraft many Nativity scene stables annually for Bronner's.) As the number of accounts grew, several part-time employees were added. In 1951, neighbor Wally Weiss assisted with the painting of signs and posters in addition to holding another full-time job. Other early helpers were Duane Pommerville and Bruce Bartlett. In the 1950s, the Bronner painting team, including Wally, painted a Master Mix Feeds sign on the top of the 100-ft.-tall Star of the West Milling Company silo in Frankenmuth.

Wally met sweetheart Irene Pretzer in 1945 through the Walther League youth activities of the Lutheran church. Wally's first major account for window decorating on a monthly basis was with Jennison Hardware Company of Bay City. The account was the result of an advantageous set of circumstances. Wally's girlfriend, Irene, attended Bay City Junior College, boarding at the home of G. W. Cooke, president of the hardware company. She was responsible for making the initial contact for Bronner Display and Sign Advertising.

Irene became a teacher in the Frankenmuth school system and began helping Wally make Christmas centerpieces for the Durant Hotel in Flint, the Bancroft Hotel in Saginaw, and the Wenona Hotel in Bay City, as well as Zehnder's and Fischer's (in later years, Bavarian Inn) restaurants in Frankenmuth.

Wally married Irene Ruth Pretzer, the daughter of William and Anna Pretzer of Hemlock, Michigan, on June 23, 1951. Irene, coincidentally, was the same size as the standard mannequin in store windows, and at times Wally dressed the mannequins in Irene's clothing.

A special opportunity arose in 1951 when Wally was trimming windows at Jennison Hardware in Bay City. Merchants from Clare, Michigan, watched him work, and then entered Jennison's store to inquire about the purchase of Christmas decorations appropriate for display on their city streets. The hardware store had none for sale, but the store manager, Lawrence Pressler, referred the gentlemen to the window trimmer for suggestions. Since Wally knew of no location where such decorations might be purchased, he offered to make Christmas panels for the Clare lampposts himself. The Clare merchants, chaired by Mr. Evart of Evart's Jewelry, agreed to the plan, and Wally, with the help of friend and Bay City sign artist Louie Priem, painted holiday designs on hardboard panels for display on the Clare, Michigan, lampposts. The project was successful; other area merchants placed orders the following year.

It occurred to Wally after additional orders that surely other cities might be interested in decorations of a similar nature. About this time (the early '50s) Wally's friend, Fred Bernthal, returned home from military service looking for a job. Wally hired him and the two visited municipal and chamber of commerce offices in Michigan, Ohio, Indiana, and Ontario cities to survey what potential there might be for street decorations in these areas. The tour was most encouraging! They discovered a large market ready and waiting. On the return trip home, Wally and Fred ordered merchandise for city street decorations from two supply houses: General Plastics Corporation in Marion, Indiana; and Mold-Craft Corporation of Port Washington, Wisconsin. General Plastics supplied pole trims and ornaments, street streamers, and illuminated greeting signs. Mold-Craft produced latex figures such as Nativity scenes, carolers, reindeer, and Santas.

Wally mailed innovative invitations inviting officials to attend a decoration exhibit in Frankenmuth. Items were displayed for prospective buyers in the spring of 1952 in the Frankenmuth Township Hall that Wally rented for the event. The showing was so successful that a second was scheduled for the fall of the same year, this time in a larger facility: the St. Lorenz School gymnasium. A high school student, Ruth Weiss, was hired as receptionist.

The painting of signs and decorative panels went hand-in-hand with the Christmas decorations division, which flourished after the initial showings in Frankenmuth.

Wally credits the fame and beauty of the Frankenmuth community, the old-world atmosphere, and the fame of Zehnder's family-style chicken dinners with helping attract guests to Bronner's showings.

The detailed work involved in preparing the exhibits and taking them down to be stored between showings led Wally to search for a place to be rented on a permanent basis. A vacated, one-room school on East Genesee Street (formerly Frankenmuth School District Number One) served such a purpose in 1952. This made a year-round exhibit of Christmas decorations possible. At first the people of the community thought the idea to be rather unusual, but later accepted it fully when Frankenmuth became known as "the Christmas town."

SHOWINGS FOR BRONNER DECORATIONS - Because the Spring 1952 showing of city decorations in Frankenmuth was so successful, a sequel was planned for Marshall, Michigan, in spring, 1953. The appeal of a free meal at famous Schulers Restaurant brought crowds that included guests from our neighboring counties.

Transporting decorations and setting up for shows was laborious and costly; therefore, we reasoned that having our own permanent year-round salesroom would be more beneficial.

The rest is history. Our first permanent location opened in 1954 - in friendly Frankenmuth.

Early Sign Work

WALLY'S FIRST SIGN. Wally copied the lettering style from the Bible.

Wally painted his **FIRST WATERCOLOR** for an art show at Zehnder's Restaurant.

Some of the early artwork is on display in **BRONNER'S PROGRAM CENTER**. In the mid '40s, Wally and helpers lettered numerous trucks, posters, and barn signs. The first truck lettered was for Paul Zuellig & Son.

Wally's first hand-lettered poster for **ED DAENZER'S BARBER SHOP**.

ROLAND GUGEL (by car) and **WALDO VANEK** (right of Wally) were early part-time helpers along with Wallace Weiss (not pictured).

Early Display Work

In the late '40s, Wally's brother Arnold, a banker, helped part-time at the Hubinger Store artistically creating window displays. **WHEN ARNOLD WAS DRAFTED INTO THE ARMY, WINDOW TRIMS BECAME WALLY'S RESPONSIBILITY** in addition to clerking.

Wally the Clerk, and inset, Arnold

Signs of the Times

BRONNER'S BUILT many floats and billboards.

4 Blocks NORTH of HOTELS

RUPPRECHT'S FRANKENMUTH SAUSAGE

Old Fashioned • HAMS • BACON

OPEN DAILY to 6 • FRIDAYS to 9 • SUNDAYS 1 to 6

37

One of Wally's early graphics was a street banner for Oxford, Michigan.

GRAPHIC PRODUCTS for Frankenmuth included a decorative greeting sign for the front of Zehnder's Restaurant; an entrance sign for the city park, and metal letters to identify a school.

In 1945 the Gera Dramatic Walther League, a youth organization of St. Lorenz Lutheran Church, gave Wally an order for **FRANKENMUTH'S FIRST, CUT-OUT, HAND-PAINTED NATIVITY SCENE** for the lawn of St. Lorenz Lutheran School on Main Street.

Wally points to his first sign for Zehnder's Restaurant. The sign is still in use.

Early Major Accounts

The first account for window displays was Jennison Hardware Store in Bay City, Michigan.

GENE GWIZDALA (left) ordered music stands for his Polka-Dots Band. Also pictured is trumpeter **GIL KOLB**.

LOUIE PRIEM hand-lettered the order of 24 panels that were designed by Wally, and built and delivered by **EDDIE BEYERLEIN** (Pictured).

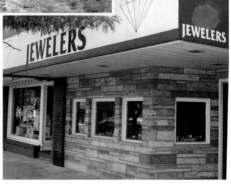

In 1951 the fledgling Bronner business received its **FIRST ORDER OF 24 LAMPPOST DECORATIONS** ($21.75 each) from merchants gathered at Everett Jewelers in **CLARE, MICHIGAN**. The "Clare County Review" featured a nostalgic article of that sale in its August 22, 2003, issue.

LOUIE PRIEM, sign artist, and **EDDIE BEYERLEIN** hand-lettered numerous barn signs. Eddie was Wally's first full-time Bronner employee.

Behind Wally is the Roth Carpenter Shop that was converted into a sign shop in the mid 1940s.

Wally's sister **HELEN BRONNER-RUPPRECHT**

During the 1940s and '50s, the **BRONNER TEAM DECORATED MANY BOOTHS AT THE SAGINAW COUNTY FAIR.** The team labored long hours to decorate more than 100 booths and supply hundreds of signs. (l to r) Wally's sister, Helen; Louie Priem; Wally's brother, Arnold; Eddie Beyerlein; Walter Hahn; Harry Hasselbeck; Wally; and Jim Gilbert.

Wedding Bells

At a 1950 District Walther League Convention in St. Joseph, Michigan, District President **WALLY PROPOSED TO SWEETHEART** and Saginaw Valley Zone President, Irene Ruth Pretzer. Irene was an elementary school music teacher.

They were married at St. Peter Lutheran Church in Hemlock, Michigan, on June 23, 1951.

Wally's parents,
ELLA and **HERMAN BRONNER**.

Irene's parents,
ANNA and **WILLIAM PRETZER**.

Christmas Decorations Shows

In 1951, Bronner's hosted a **SPRING SHOWING** of outdoor Christmas decorations in the Frankenmuth Township Hall. The showing was so successful that a **FALL SHOW** was held in the gymnasium of St. Lorenz School in Frankenmuth.

The showing featured lamppost decorations, street streamers, and garlands.

On the ladder is part-time helper, **BRUCE BARTLETT**, with **WALLY BRONNER** and **FRED BERNTHAL**, Bronner's first, part-time sales representative.

THE FIRST, YEAR-ROUND SALESROOM in 1952 was a rented two-room schoolhouse on East Genesee Street.

42

Early Promotional Items

FIRST CATALOG for the Bronner Business was produced in 1953.

the BRONNER line
CHRISTMAS DECORATIONS
STREETS - BUILDINGS - PARKS
FRONT YARDS - INTERIORS

DESIGNERS - PRODUCERS - DISTRIBUTORS

BRONNER DISPLAY & SIGN ADVERTISING
290 Haas St. — Frankenmuth, Michigan — Dial 2271

SEASON'S GREETINGS

No. BCOL-23 — Season's Greetings Cut-Out Letters.

WALLACE J. BRONNER
FRANKENMUTH, MICH.
DIAL 2271

BRONNER
Displays & Signs
Commercial Artist

WINDOW & INTERIOR
DISPLAY SERVICE

SIGNS OF ANY DESCRIPTION

TRUCK LETTERING

ADVERTISING IDEAS

BUSINESS CARDS used prior to first permanent location.

INDOOR AND OUTDOOR
CHRISTMAS DECORATIONS

BRONNER
DISPLAY
AND **SIGN**
Advertising

● DESIGNERS
● PRODUCERS
● DISTRIBUTORS

WALLACE J. BRONNER
FRANKENMUTH, MICHIGAN
290 HAAS ST.   DIAL 2272

● DESIGNERS   of Indoor - Outdoor
● PRODUCERS
● DISTRIBUTORS
CHRISTMAS and ALL SEASONS DECORATIONS
DISPLAY MATERIALS ● SIGNS ● EXHIBITS

BRONNER
DISPLAY & SIGN ADVERTISING, INC.
FRANKENMUTH, MICH., 121 E. TUSCOLA
(Over)

Wally Bronner
President — Manager

OLive 2-2271

FIRST BUSINESS CARD at time of first permanent location.

43

Wally's First Accounting Book

FIRST ACCOUNTING BOOK - Wally was 12 years old when he began keeping his first accounting book, a 3.5" x 5.5" spiral, which lists entries beginning with April 27, 1939. The book, which is still in good condition, notes tips of 1¢ to 25¢ that Wally received for making bicycle deliveries of bread baked in an outdoor brick oven by Wally's mother Ella, Aunt Hattie Hubinger, and Grandma Maria Hubinger. The round loaves of bread sold for 14¢.

4 | The First Permanent Location

Wally's father, contractor Herman Bronner, recognized his son's need for a permanent building in which to carry on his business and offered to build it for him. The location chosen was 121 East Tuscola Street, the lot adjoining what was then Wally's Aunt Hattie Hubinger's grocery store. (The lot had formerly served as Hattie's vegetable and flower garden. It was originally purchased from the United States government by Wally's great-grandfather, Johann Mathias Hubinger.) Wally's sketches for the building showed two rectangular buildings joined to form an L-shaped structure. After studying the sketches, his father made the suggestion that, with little extra cost, the building could be made much larger if it were square-shaped. Wally wasn't at all sure he had use for the additional space, but agreed to go along with his father's ideas. Wally is ever thankful for his father's advice, vision, and business loan.

Wally's mother, Ella Hubinger Bronner, and his Aunt Hattie approved of Wally's career in display and sign work, encouraging him in every way. They showed great interest in plans for the new building, but regretfully Wally's mother did not live to see its completion. She was called to her heavenly home in early 1954.

Wally's uncles were in the masonry contracting business. They had learned this skill from their father, John (Johann), a German immigrant. Together, they operated their business under the name Bronner Brothers. Herman Bronner and his brother Richard constructed the 3,600 square-foot building at 121 Tuscola Street, completing it in the fall of 1954. One half was allocated to sign painting while the other half served as a display area for Christmas trims, also included was a Ratskeller-themed meeting room that overlooked the Cass River.

During the first two or three months of the year, the part devoted to Christmas displays was closed off to conserve heat.

When the warm weather returned, it was opened for the few curious people who wandered through. A record player with 76-RPM records provided background Christmas music during the occasional customer visits.

As city representatives came to Bronner's to order decorations, they also looked for trims suitable for their own establishments. As a result, decorations for stores, shopping centers, parking lots, malls, and commercial interiors were added to Bronner's offerings. A complete line of religious decorations, particularly for churches, was also added, enabling customers to offer a visual witness to the real meaning of Christmas.

As couples selected decorations for their stores and churches, the wives, often accompanying their husbands on such buying trips, requested decorations for their homes. By 1960, a complete line of decorations and gifts for the home had been added.

Edna Martens, who started working for Bronner's in 1958, became the first full-time salesroom manager. She served in that capacity until 1977 when she retired.

From 1954 through 1963, Bronner's annually featured an attractive exhibit of Christmas decorations at the Saginaw County Fair. This exposure greatly helped to publicize the company since annual fair attendance during those years reached over 300,000.

During the early '50s, Saginaw display specialist Jim Gilbert and Wally combined forces to decorate booths at the Fair. Lou Taylor from the Michigan Bean Company engaged Wally to decorate a booth (Wally's first) at the Saginaw County Fair.

In 1954 Jim became Bronner's first full-time sales representative, selling Christmas decorations to towns, cities, and chambers of commerce. Jim gave Bronner's nearly 30 years of dedicated service.

During this era, Frankenmuth began to follow the Bavarian theme in architectural decor. The peaked roofs, stucco, wood trim, and decorative shutters are prominent architectural features in portions of Bavaria and in the Alpine mountain regions of Germany, Austria, Switzerland, and northern Italy. Edmund "Ed" Arnold, editor of the "Frankenmuth News" at the time, promoted the Bavarian concept as a theme for Frankenmuth. He encouraged the community to build on its heritage; to promote German architecture, music, and festivals; and to preserve and further German traditions and cultures. Former postmaster Fred Zehnder is believed to have been the first citizen to add the Bavarian touch to a city building when he called on Wally for ornate shutters and flower boxes to decorate the post office. (While on military duty in Bavaria during World War II, Fred admired the Alpine architecture and abundance of flowers in window boxes and landscapes.)

During the mid '50s, Wally made sketches for building-front additions to Rupprecht Brothers sausage establishment, introducing Bavarian/Alpine design. Also during this time, the Zehnder family purchased the Fischer Hotel and converted the building, now known as the Frankenmuth Bavarian Inn Restaurant, to the Alpine style. William "Tiny" Zehnder, Jr. was appointed manager, and his wife Dorothy, a former waitress at Fischer's, became chief cook. At the request of Fred Zehnder, Wally sketched designs for the converted structure, and it became the pace-setter for the "Alpine look" that later became the popular theme of the community now known as "Michigan's Little Bavaria."

In 1962 a committee consisting of Rudy LaRiviere, Carl Geyer, Doris Voorheis, and Wally Bronner was appointed by Mayor Elmer Simon to design an official crest for the historic town of Frankenmuth. The crest was officially adopted by the city council in 1963. It was printed by Bronner's, marking the initiation of three-color, screen-process printing and what was years later to become Bronner Screen Printing, Inc.

Bronner's first co-op student from Frankenmuth High School was Larry Huber, who came to Bronner's in 1957 to assist in the sign shop. Also in 1957 Donald Fischer, hired as a part-time employee, was so deeply interested in the work that he stayed on the job sixty hours during his first week. His creative, artistic, and technical abilities were the key to his advancement in the business over a period of years — from the position of part-time employee to general manager of the display and sign division.

The entire business was incorporated in 1960 under the name Bronner Display and Sign Advertising, Inc., with Clarence Siers of Yeo & Yeo PC CPA as accounting and business adviser, Robert Stroebel as legal adviser, and Frankenmuth State Bank as financial adviser. The board of directors included Wally as President and Treasurer, Irene as Vice President and Secretary, and Arnold Bronner (Wally's brother) as board member.

The development of shopping centers and malls established a need for a display specialist to serve such accounts. Dick Schluckbier became the first full-time employee to serve in that capacity in 1961. In the early 1960s, displays for introducing color phones were supplied by Bronner's to business offices for Michigan Bell and Rocky Mountain Bell Telephone Companies.

Wally has always appreciated his father's foresight in recommending the construction of a larger building than he first envisioned. Not only was all the extra space utilized, but more ground floor space and a second story were also added in 1963 for expanded product lines and storage. Since his father had entered his heavenly abode in 1960, Wally's uncle, William Bronner, and Wally's cousin Ron were contracted to build this addition.

Eventually, the Bronner business outgrew the building on Tuscola Street, even with its addition. In 1964, Wally and Irene purchased additional property from Hattie Hubinger for a parking lot to accommodate the growing number of guests.

In 1953, Wally's father Herman said, "**SKETCH A PICTURE OF THE BUILDING** that you would like for your sign and display business." Herman drew the building plans from the illustration.

AUNT HATTIE offered to sell her floral garden plot and bake-oven on the corner of Tuscola and Main Streets for the building site.

Hubinger's General Store's **HISTORIC BAKE-OVEN** on the backside of the property was razed to make room for the new structure.

49

HERMAN BRONNER'S WORK CREW and Wally's part-time helpers combined their skills to complete the building.

HERMAN BRONNER adapted the limestone design on part of the building from a residence on Superior Street in Saginaw, Michigan. Decorative, slender, Roman-style bricks and cut limestone were used for the decorative building front.

The "Frankenmuth News" featured a photo of **WALLY** and **HIS FATHER** during the fall 1954 opening.

Doors Open
1954

Holiday lighting added brilliance to the building's exterior.

GUESTS ENJOYED THE VAST ARRAY of indoor and outdoor trims for residential and commercial use.

The **1954 CHRISTMAS GREETING CARD** was hand-lettered by Wally. (l to r: **OLGA NUECHTERLEIN**; **WALLY BRONNER**; **FRED BERNTHAL**; and **HENRY BENDER, JR.**)

Graphics

Bronner's produced billboards for many customers. **"WE WERE OUR OWN BEST CUSTOMER."**

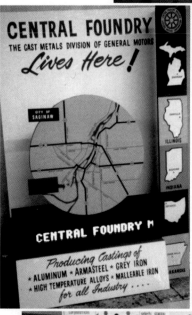

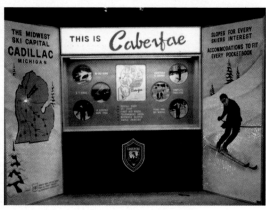

Numerous portable exhibits were produced in the 1950s and '60s.

EDUCATIONAL CHARTS were hand-lettered by **MARV JAHNKE** (second from right). **HENRY BENDER** (far right) and **EDDIE BEYERLEIN** (far left) installed the displays at General Motors Institute of Technology in Flint, Michigan. **HERMAN BRONNER** (second from left) smilingly approved of the graphic products in his son's new business.

52

More Graphics

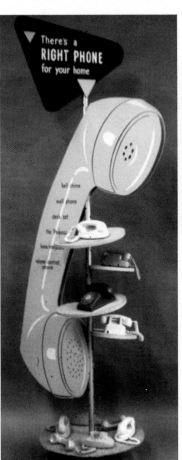

SEASONAL POINT-OF-PURCHASE DISPLAYS were built for the regional offices of the Michigan Bell Telephone Company and Mountain States Telephone Company.

CUTOUT LETTERS galore were supplied for holiday messages for parks, building fronts, and street banners.

Moldcraft Corporation of Wisconsin supplied figurines for displayers produced by Bronner's.

53

THE EARLY 1960s BRONNER STAFF were front row (l to r): "Fritzie" Hill, Sally (Sohn) Loesel, Edith Zeilinger, Sue Weiss, Doris Voorheis, Sophie Marcet, and Edna Martens. Back row (l to r): Larry Huber; Henry Bender, Jr.; Don Fischer; Eddie Beyerlein; Fred Beyerlein; Lewis Simpson; Marv Jahnke; Jim Gilbert; and Wally.

Greeting panels, carolers, ornaments, and Nativity scenes were customer favorites.

Outdoor decorations for homes became popular.

Early Suppliers of Christmas Trims

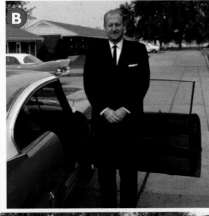

F **RON KOWALSKI** (not pictured) of R.K. International was a pioneer in producing animated figures.

A) Wally with founder **HENRY ERLEWINE**, engineer **CHARLES RICHTER**, and President **RICHARD ERLEWINE** of General Plastics Corporation in Marion, Indiana; B) **MATT OFFEN** of Valley Decorating, Fresno, California; C) **LEW WILLIAMS** of L.C. Williams Company, Houston, Texas; D) **BOB METZGER** of Frederick Displays International in Chicago, Illinois; E) **DAVID HAMBERGER** of Hamberger Animation, New York City, New York; and G) the **WILKINSONS** from North American Evergreen, Cook, Minnesota.

The first billboard outside Frankenmuth was on the triangular-shaped Clock Tower Building in downtown Saginaw, Michigan. Just like **TIMES SQUARE** in New York City.

Buyers **EDNA MARTENS** and **DORIS REDA** in Rockefeller Center, New York City, during a buying trip with Wally.

A growing number of **TOUR GROUPS, BUYING COMMITTEES, and CHRISTMAS DECORATION ENTHUSIASTS** were amazed at the vast selection Bronner buyers brought to Frankenmuth from New York and overseas markets.

56

Party Time!

The dedicated staff enjoyed working together as well as socializing at annual and semiannual get-togethers.

1957 - (Front row) Jane Beyerlein, Barb Beyerlein, Marge Beyerlein, Ellen Bender, Doris Voorheis, Irene Bronner, Fritzie Hill, Peggy Vitany (Second row) Andy Vitany, Fred Voorheis, Sue Weiss, Charlotte Jahnke, Helen Gilbert, Olga Nuechterlein, Wally Bronner (Third row) Fred Beyerlein, Jim Gilbert, Marv Jahnke, Don Fischer, Eddie Beyerlein, Bill Hill, Henry Bender, Ossie Nuechterlein, Larry Huber, Gilbert Weiss

1959 - (Front row) Edna Martens, Sue Weiss, Fritzie Hill, Doris Voorheis, Peggy Vitany (Second row) Marv Jahnke, Erna Eberlein, Pate Gower, Larry Huber, Jim Gilbert (Third row) Eddie Beyerlein, Don Fischer, Fred Beyerlein, Wally Bronner

1964 - (Front row) Karen Fischer, Ruth Schluckbier, Marie Fulco, Ellen Bender, Jan Eisler, Doris Reda, Irene Bronner, Randy Bronner, Carla Bronner (Second row) Henry Bender, Frank Fulco, Helen Gilbert, Marge Beyerlein, Sophie Marcet, Edna Martens, Kay Finkbeiner, Wayne Bronner (Third row) Dick Schluckbier, Derwood Finkbeiner, Martha Huber, Jim Gilbert, Fritzie Hill, Jeanne Borcherding, Erna Eberlein, Fred Gower, Pate Gower, Lowell Borcherding (Fourth row) Marco Marcet, Fred Beyerlein, Fred Reda, Ruben Mossner, Roy Martens, Larry Huber, Eddie Beyerlein, Dorothy Mossner, Bill Hill, Wyman Eberlein

Commercial Decorating Committees

FIRST PERMANENT LOCATION

CITY OF DETROIT delegation, greeted by Wally, visited frequently.

DORIS VOORHEIS (left) and **SHIRLEY (ANDREWS) GREEN**.

ON STAFF IN 1962 were front row (l to r): Don Fischer, Doris Reda, Sally (Sohn) Loesel, Sue Weiss, Sophie Marcet, and Eddie Beyerlein. Second row: Fred Gower, Patronella Gower, Erna Eberlein, and Fred Beyerlein. Third row: Frank Fulco; Edna Martens; Edith Zeilinger; and Henry Bender, Jr. Fourth row: Jim Gilbert, Fritzie Hill, and Dick Schluckbier. Fifth row: Carrol Nuechterlein, Lewis Simpson, and Wally Schluckebier. Sixth row: Marv Jahnke and Larry Huber. Top: Wally Bronner.

Christmas Scenes in the 1960s

MARION,
Indiana

DETROIT,
Michigan

Camera-ready Wally!

FLINT, Michigan

DEARBORN (Michigan) City Hall

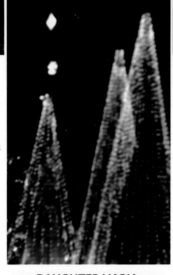

GIGANTIC STYLIZED TREES graced the Coleman A. Young Detroit City County Building in Detroit, Michigan.

Illuminated **POLE DECORATIONS** made of plastic, fiberglass, and foil added dazzle to the décor.

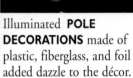

Wally and Irene's youngest **DAUGHTER MARIA** was awed at the sight of the Santa, sleigh and reindeer fiberglass figures added in the 1960s to the Bronner product line.

60

First Major Display

ROBERT (BOB) WILSON, Midland, Mich.

BOB chaired the committee of **GIL CURRIE**, **LEONARD BERGSTEIN** and **DIRK WALTZ** that engaged Bronner's to supply a spectacular Christmas display for the Midland County Courthouse lawn.

All original sketches by **DON FISCHER**...early 1960s.

The display is an annual attraction. It was a major undertaking for Midland and Bronner's.

Bronner's 15-ft. and 6-ft. **FIBERGLASS SNOWMEN** are popular park and shopping center trims.

61

1963 Expansion

...tripled the salesroom and sign production area and added second floor storage.

After Wally's dad died in 1960, Uncle **BILL BRONNER AND SON RON** were the general contractors.

Grandpa Gottfried Hubinger's barn, next to the shop, had served as a warehouse but was razed for the expansion.

Visit **BRONNER'S OF FRANKENMUTH, MICH.**

See **AMERICA'S LARGEST YEAR-AROUND DISPLAY OF CHRISTMAS DECORATIONS**

A mid-1960s postcard of the enlarged salesroom.

Pylons and Billboards

WICKES was our first nationwide account. One large order of billboards included 40 miles of white slats when laid end-to-end.

Revolving sign for Flint, MI, restaurant owned by Arni and Fran Walli.

The first Frankenmuth Crest was designed in 1963 by (l to r) **WALLY, DORIS VOORHEIS, CARL GEYER,** and **RUDY LA RIVIERE** (not pictured).

In 2001, the community honored national journalist **EDMUND ARNOLD**, 1940s editor of the "Frankenmuth News," for suggesting a Bavarian theme for Frankenmuth.

The emblems for Frankenmuth's 125th year were screen-printed at Bronner's under the supervision of **DON FISCHER**.

FRED and **LORENE ZEHNDER** promoted Bavarian attire, dirndls, and lederhosen for Frankenmuth's first Bavarian Festival in 1959. During the early years, **FRED** and **WALLY** served as emcees for the festival.

BOB REINDEL (left) and **AL KOSCHE** (right) met with many customers to serve sign, exhibit, and screen-printing needs.

BOB WEISS prepared shipments of signs for Saudi Arabia.

FAMILY CRESTS were supplied during the 1950s and '60s.

MANY BILLBOARDS were painted in the expansive building addition.

64

Commercial Trims

JIM GILBERT and two decoration committee members from Sylvania, Ohio, pose in front of Bronner's new 17-ft. Santa.

A trio of sales specialists for commercial Christmas decorations: (l to r) **DICK SCHLUCKBIER, JIM GILBERT,** and **LANNY NUECHTERLEIN**.

The **SIGN DEPARTMENT** and **CHRISTMAS DEPARTMENT** enjoyed annual Christmas parties, alternating between Zehnder's Restaurant and the Bavarian Inn. Pictured is the **1973 BRONNER GROUP**. In later years, to accommodate the growing staff, separate parties were held for the Sign and Christmas staffs and their spouses.

MARTHA DIXON, WJIM, LANSING - The "Martha Dixon Show" on WJIM in Lansing provided Wally his first major opportunity for television coverage. He was an annual guest on the program's Christmas kickoff the day after Thanksgiving during the mid '50s.

PRIVATE PLANE VISITORS - After Bronner's completed its building in the '50s and '60s, buyers from Sears' headquarters in Chicago visited. The display buyers arrived by private plane in Flint where Wally met them. They ordered a Bronner fiberglass Nativity scene.

VISITS FROM THE GIANTS - Buyers from Firestone, Sears, and Kmart have visited Bronner's.

INTERNATIONAL BUYERS - Store managers and buyers from England, the Netherlands, Germany, Australia and other nations have visited Bronner's.

LARGE CHECK RECEIVED - Bronner's received a check for $177,996 in 1973 when the screen-printing division produced an order of silhouette-style tool boards for numerous automobile dealers throughout the USA.

BRONNER'S ANNUAL TIDINGS - newsletter was first published in 1976 when the business relocated from city center to the south side of Frankenmuth.

Rudy Petzold, editor of the "Tuscola County Advertiser" was the graphic artist and copy writer. Rudy advised, "Always use many photos."

5 | The Business Blossoms

After attending his first International Trade Fair in Europe in 1965, Wally initiated direct importing of Christmas merchandise. That same year Bronner's rented a building formerly known as the Ken Theatre Building, which they utilized for storage.

Business continued to mushroom. The Frankenmuth Bank building, located across the street from the main showroom at the northeast corner of Main Street and East Tuscola Street, was vacated in 1966. Wally and Irene purchased the structure and converted it into the Tannenbaum (German for Christmas tree) Shop. It featured a wide variety of artificial Christmas trees; garlands; wreaths; and artistic, hand-painted, blown-glass ornaments for tree trimming and was managed by Doris Reda. (She worked for Aunt Hattie when the Hubinger Grocery Store was still in operation.) Harry O. Meyer, doorman for the Tannenbaum Shop, had a special way of greeting guests who appeared hesitant to climb the five steps to the front door. "Welcome, young ladies," or "young men" definitely seemed to add a bounce to their step. (In later years Harry also served as a Santa Claus helper.)

Because of the burgeoning business and the large shipments arriving from overseas, additional storage places around town were secured. The Bronners purchased the Engel family home (adjacent to the Tannenbaum Shop) and rented a corner of the Star of the West Milling Co. warehouse, a section of the Baker Automobile Sales warehouse, and an area in the Frankenmuth Woolen Mill. From 1945 to 2000, Bronner's occupied showroom and storage space in over 30 different buildings in various locations throughout Frankenmuth.

It became increasingly obvious that consolidation of showroom and storage areas under one roof was inevitable. Planning for the construction of such a facility, the Bronners followed a suggestion made by Herbert Keinath, city manager at the time, and bought a large, triangular-shaped, 50-acre parcel of land on the south side of Frankenmuth. The acreage was acquired from owners Henry and Bertha Conzelmann (1965), Herbert and Renata List (1966), and Harold and Marcella Weber (1969). Wally and Irene regarded this property as "space insurance," looking toward the 1970s when they hoped to construct a building large enough to take care of all of the business' needs.

For history's sake, it must be said that Herbert Keinath was a visionary city manager. The idea of relocating the business must be credited to Herb. The 50-acre tract of land came to the Bronner family through exceptional circumstances as each of the three prior owners decided to sell his plot of land. The Bronner family is most grateful to the sellers because the land, which seemed too huge of an investment at the time, became ideal for future expansion. Wally and Irene often comment that God seemingly sent special angels and blessings to them via City Manager Keinath and the Conzelmanns, Lists, and Webers.

In the early '70s the Bronner's sold approximately five acres to Walter and Maria Palmer. They erected and operated an impressive and popular Bavarian-themed motel.

The year 1968 was a time of decision for the display and sign division of the Bronner business. At the time, Bronner's production of highway billboards was about equal to that of point-of-sale displays and exhibits. After attending hearings on the controversial federal highway beautification legislation, Bronner's decided to allow the larger billboard companies to pursue the challenge and to turn their full attention to the expansion of the display and sign business.

In 1966 camera and dark-room facilities had been added to the screen-printing facilities. New, automated screen-printing was added in 1968 to the line of services, making possible mass production of signs (versus the one-at-a-time procedure). This division of the business was moved to a building located directly behind the Edelweiss Restaurant, owned by Ray and Roberta Weiss.

In January 1969, Bronner's experienced a fire that damaged the front lobby in the main showroom and did considerable smoke damage to merchandise. Miraculously, the fire, which started during the night, extinguished itself due to lack of oxygen, preventing a possible catastrophe.

Bronner's originally distributed a life-size and half life-size, latex Nativity scene produced by Mold-craft in Port Washington, Wisconsin. In the early '60s, a disastrous fire burned the entire Mold-craft factory. Only hand-carved wooden sets or statuary marble or plaster sets were available in the larger Nativity sizes. Many of them were not ideal for outdoor use and were very expensive. Because of Bronner's belief that a Nativity scene, especially an outdoor one, serves as a visual witness to remind viewers of the significance of CHRISTmas, the Bronner's wanted to be able to offer a life-size, outdoor Nativity that would be more affordable.

For a time, BRONNER'S CHRISTmas WONDERLAND sold a fiberglass set produced by George Tirone Studios in Boston. Still, it was Wally Bronner's dream to offer a life-size, moderately-priced Nativity scene that would have the Christ child molded right into the manger to prevent the removal of the Christ child as a prank. Wally also wanted life-size, standing camels and wisemen to complete the set, and he wanted their garments and accessories to be molded into each piece.

The Bronner dream was realized in 1969 when a life-size, 17-figure, fiberglass Nativity scene was developed in cooperation with two Italian artists and sculptors, George Tirone and Luigi Mucci, from the Boston area. Wally patented the fiberglass molds to preserve their uniqueness and identify them as Bronner exclusives.

The first complete set was sold to a volunteer church group for the Hastings, Michigan, city park. Wally and Jim (Gilbert) served as speakers at the dedication.

After a Tirone Studio fire in the mid-'70s destroyed Bronner's exclusive molds, John DeStefano and Sons from Woburn, Massachusetts, re-sculpted the figures and continued their production. In the mid-'90s, the DeStefano studios discontinued business and Bronner's began handling the production of the fiberglass sets, with the actual painting of the figures taking place at Bronner's.

Throughout the '60s and '70s, Bronner's continued to grow. In 1971, Aunt Hattie Hubinger entered her heavenly home. Wally and Irene purchased her grocery store (next to Bronner's Main Showroom) and converted it into a third salesroom named Bronner's Bavarian Corner. The Bronner business now filled three adjacent salesrooms: the Main Showroom, the Tannenbaum Shop, and the Bavarian Corner. Bronner's Bavarian Corner featured Hummel figurines; a wide selection of steins and decanters; gift items from Bavaria and other countries around the world; and ornate, hand-carved candles. Shirley Brodowski, a longtime staff member, managed this salesroom.

Also in 1971, Bronner's expanded the variety of ornaments produced in Europe. Currently, nearly 50 percent of the glass ornaments sold at BRONNER'S CHRISTmas WONDERLAND are Bronner's own designs. Doris Reda, a talented Bronner manager who retired in 1999, and Connie Larsen, a Bronner's staff artist, have designed the majority of Bronner-exclusive ornaments for production in Europe. The ornaments are designed at Bronner's, and then the artwork is sent overseas to be produced by glass artisans in Germany, Austria, Italy, Poland, the Czech Republic, Slovakia, Hungary, and Pacific Rim nations. Some are also produced in the USA. A great number of these original designs are religious-oriented, featuring angels, stars, the Holy Family, scripture texts, and carols.

In 1973 the Bronner family (Wally, Irene, Wayne, Carla, Randy and Maria) went on a buying trip to Europe so that they might become acquainted with the whole spectrum of suppliers whom Wally had searched out since his first trip in 1965.

The next year saw an expansion of the resale department and customer service. The sale of homestyle Christmas decorations to retailers, who offered Bronner items in their stores, started in the late 1950s. The first sales were to the Bintz Apple Mountain Gift Shop in Freeland, Michigan, which purchased items such as bells, garlands, and ribbons to arrange into decorative doors, swags, wreaths, and garlands. As Bronner's product line grew, so did the number of resale accounts. Bronner's direct importing of European glass ornaments, including Bronner's own designs, opened additional avenues of distribution.

As the general public became aware that Bronner's custom designed ornaments, requests began coming from fundraising organizations, churches, educational institutions, and communities that were giving recognition to a 25-, 50-, or 100-year plateau. Through the years, Bronner's art department has designed a wide array of custom ornaments and the demand is still growing. The Ladies Guild of Valparaiso University, under the leadership of Mary Ellen Simon, was one of the first major customers in 1975.

BRONNER'S CHRISTmas WONDERLAND has served many well-known people throughout the years, but all guests receive the same courteous treatment. However, it was with a certain special satisfaction that staff members filled an order (received December 15, 1976) from John Wayne, who asked for the best Santa Claus suit "with a natural-appearing wig and beard." Wally had the privilege of receiving that phone call from "the Duke."

Bronner's three stores became so crowded on fall weekends in the '70s that it was necessary to hire doormen on weekends to control the lines of people waiting to enter. The intersection by the stores became congested with motorists and pedestrians. There were not enough restrooms to service all the guests, especially when a series of motorcoaches unloaded. Inside the stores, shopping conditions were very crowded. More space was needed.

Bronner's Screen Printing, with ten employees, hired their first full-time salesman, Al Kosche in 1974. Al spread the word that Bronner Display had screen-printing capabilities which equaled that of Detroit printers. Although the nation was experiencing an economic recession, the year 1975 saw definite growth in the business. Orders for 250,000 snowmobile and boat registration decals for the State of Michigan bolstered production. Tool-guide boards, screened on plastic, were produced and shipped to the majority of automobile dealerships in the USA.

Direct Importing from Europe Began in 1965

Wally met Christmas tree ornament producers **MARTHA** and **HEINZ MATTHAI** at an international trade fair in Nuremberg, Germany. They produced the first Bronner-designed Nativity scene ornament.

Bronner buyers have made frequent overseas trips. The Statue of Liberty is always a welcome sight on the homebound trip.

Customs broker, **FRANK COUGHLIN**, and Wally inspected the decorations cargo that arrived from Europe in the port of Detroit.

During a 1954 Walther League group tour, Wally and Irene met **JOHN WAYNE** at Zion National Park. In 1976, John Wayne purchased a Santa suit from Bronner's.

72

Bronner Family Visits
European Suppliers

The family at the site of the Iron Curtain in 1973 near Coburg, Germany.

SON WAYNE received a glassblowing lesson in Germany

The **DE CARLINI FAMILY** in the Como region of Northern Italy produces artistic, figural glass ornaments.

EUROPEAN ALPINE ARCHITECTURE influenced the design for the Bronner buildings.

In 1978, buyers **ANNE KOEHLER** (l) and **CARLA BRONNER** (r) with a De Carlini artisan.

73

In 1966...

Bronner's opened the **TANNENBAUM SHOP** in the former Frankenmuth State Bank building located across the street from the Main Salesroom and facing Main Street.

The array of trees decorated in religious, traditional, and toyland themes impressed a growing number of visitors.

Decorator and ornament designer **DORIS REDA** managed the new store.

Fiberglass Figures

In 1969 Bronner's commissioned Italian artisans from the George Tirone Studios in Boston to sculpt Christmas-themed figures from which molds were made and patented.

GEORGE TIRONE, owner, **SCULPTOR LUIGI MUCCI**, and **JOSEPHINE COSEMINI**, office manager.

Original sculptures of a **BRONNER NATIVITY**

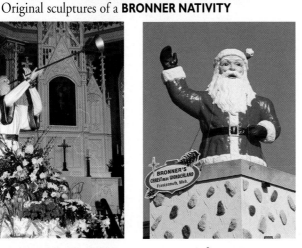

4-ft. **CANTERBURY CAROLERS**

9-ft. **TRUMPETING ANGEL**

17-ft. **SANTA**

Production was moved to the studios of **JOHN DESTEFANO** in Wolburn, Massachusetts, after a devastating fire at the George Tirone Studio in the 1970s.

Nativity scenes depict the reason for the CHRISTmas season.

The majestic, colorful, weatherproof fiberglass set was introduced in 1969.

Bronner's 17-Piece Lifesize Nativity Scene

Shipments have been made to five continents for use by churches, Christmas spectaculars, parks, businesses, parade floats, and homes.

Nativity Scene Settings

THE BUSINESS BLOSSOMS

**DOWNTOWN
DETROIT**,
Renaissance
Towers in
background.

**ST. MICHAEL'S LUTHERAN
CHURCH**, Richville
(Frankenhilf), Michigan.

78

St. Luke's Hospital (now **COVENANT MEDICAL CENTER**), Saginaw, Michigan.

The **BROOKS FOUNTAIN** colonnades in Marshall, Michigan, provide a unique setting for the nativity scene under a canopy of lights and stars.

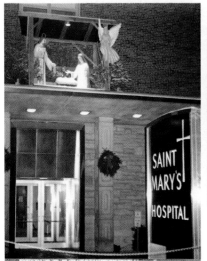

ST. MARY'S HOSPITAL, Saginaw, Michigan.

DOMINO FARMS display, Ann Arbor, Michigan.

EDWIN L. ZEHNDER PARK in Frankenmuth, Michigan.

ST. LORENZ LUTHERAN CHURCH, Frankenmuth, Michigan.

79

Bronner's Bavarian Corner
Opens in 1971

The former **AUNT HATTIE HUBINGER GROCERY STORE**, which was next door to the Main Salesroom, was converted into a shop featuring Hummel figurines, candles, pictures, nutcrackers, steins, and European-themed gifts.

GRAND OPENING DAY

(l to r) Edna Martens, Shirley Brodowski, June Auernhammer, Doris Reda, Irene and Wally Bronner.

U.S. CUSTOMS OFFICER LLOYD VEST cleared a container shipment from Europe at Bronner's with **EDDIE BEYERLEIN** and **EDNA MARTENS**.

Ornament Producers

VOLKER, WALTRAUD, and son **NORBERT WRATSCHKO**, Austrian glass ornament artisans, produced Bronner's first custom ornament of the Valparaiso Chapel, commissioned by the Ladies Guild of Valparaiso University in Valparaiso, Indiana, in 1975.

Irene and Wally toasted **WILMA** and **HELMUT KREBS** in Bavaria. The Krebs artisans are producers of elegant ornaments.

Italian artisan handpainted ornaments in assembly-line fashion. Bronner artist **FRANK FULCO** personalized the ornaments for astronauts Neil Armstrong, Buzz Aldrin, and Michael Collins to commemorate their 1969 flight to the moon. Astronaut glass ornaments were produced in Italy.

HEINZ and **INGE MÜLLER-BLECH** and their son **KLAUS** are from a long line of Lauscha ornament producers. Glass ornaments originated in Lauscha, Germany, in 1847.

Ausgabe Nr. 5   Frühjahr 1989

WEIHNACHTS-MARKT

S. 11 • CHRISTmas WONDERLAND

S. 28 • Aus dem Erzgebirge

Die Fachpublikation für Oster- und Weihnachtsschmuck

Interviews · Produktvorstellungen · Fachberichte

Hersteller-Berichte · Messe-Termine · Einzelhandel-Portraits · Buchbesprechungen

KLAUS MÜLLER-BLECH, a public relations and marketing specialist, featured a story on Bronner's CHRISTmas Wonderland in his 5th Edition, Spring 1989 publication *"WEIHNACHTSMARKT"* (Christmas Market).

Screen Printing Division Expands

Larger and faster equipment was housed in the **EDELWEISS BUILDING** on the south side of Frankenmuth.

LARRY HUBER (foreground), **HAROLD LARSEN** (background), and **BOB REINDEL** inspected production line.

BOB WEISS operated the machine for slicing screen printed products.

The needs of customers were varied.

Off-Site Buildings

... for rented storage

A corner of the **STAR OF THE WEST WAREHOUSE**.

KEN THEATRE building located on East Jefferson Street.

ZEHNDER AUTOMOBILE DEALERSHIP body shop. Wholesale orders were shipped from this location.

A portion of the **FRANKENMUTH WOOLEN MILL** warehouse.

In 1966 the Bronners purchased **DR.** and **MRS. AUGUST ENGEL'S** residence located north of the Tannenbaum Shop on Main Street, for more warehouse space.

The Need to Relocate!

CITY MANAGER HERB KEINATH observed the growing number of visitors. Visionary Herb suggested Wally and Irene consider relocating their business to the southern edge of the city.

On many weekends there were long lines at all three locations - the **MAIN SALESROOM, BAVARIAN CORNER, AND TANNENBAUM SHOP**, which necessitated a doorman at each shop to control crowds.

85

THREE SITES TO BECOME ONE. A) Bronner's Main Showroom - 1954 B) Bronner's Tannenbaum Shop - 1966 C) Bronner's Bavarian Corner - 1971

Property Purchased

REROUTING OF THE HIGHWAY AT THE SOUTH END OF FRANKENMUTH MADE AN IDEAL LOCATION. During a seven-year period, the 50-acre (20.6 hectacres), triangular plot was purchased from three landowners: the Harry and Bertha Conzelmann family, the Herb and Renata List family, and Harold and Marcella Weber.

ELLEN (Conzelmann) **FELGNER**

RUDY LIST and his twin sisters, **MARIE** and **MARGARET**

HAROLD and **MARCELLA WEBER**

6 | Bronner's Relocates to 25 Christmas Lane

Realizing that the time had come for relocation, Wally and Irene sold the Main Showroom, the Bavarian Corner, the Tannenbaum Shop, and the Engel house in 1975 to Star of the West Milling Company, managed by Richard Krafft, a school friend of Wally's. The transaction was mutually beneficial because the growing milling company also needed space.

In preparation for this relocation, Wally photographed and sketched structures that he found attractive and functional during his travels, and collected ideas that could be incorporated in the projected facility. Employees were encouraged to contribute suggestions; many of their ideas became realities.

A deadline for the availability of natural gas for commercial use accelerated construction at Bronner's new location. By deadline time, Bronner's had complied by having two cement pads and furnaces in place in an empty field.

Plans called for two buildings: one to house the screen-printing business and the other to serve primarily as a salesroom for Christmas decorations. The screen-printing building, covering 18,000 square feet, was completed during the USA bicentennial year 1976 on the property Bronner's had purchased during the 1960s on the south end of Frankenmuth.

The architect for the two buildings was Tom Schmidt; the building contractor was Ron Bronner, Wally's cousin; and the mechanical engineer was Rao Manyam. Total cost of the all-new Christmas headquarters was one and three-quarters million dollars. With the cost of the Bronner screen-printing building, the investment totaled two-and-a-half million dollars, which was financed through bank loans and insurance plans. John Metzger and Franklin Rittmueller were the helpful Frankenmuth State Bank officials.

The architecture of the Christmas building was Alpine, featuring bellcots and a slate-red roof. Flags of over 80 different countries were installed on the parking lot poles and building gables, accenting the international emphasis of the business. The interior was designed to give the impression of an Alpine village, its cluster of shops readied for yuletide.

"Tree-topping" parties for the construction workers and building material suppliers were held at the screen-printing and Christmas buildings after the roofs were completed on both. According to central European custom, the builder places an evergreen tree on the building's peak when the roof is completed. This serves as a suggestion to the building owner to provide the construction crew with snacks and beverages to show appreciation. For the Bronner topping party, the contractor contributed live trees in tubs and placed them on the roofs. Those trees were "recycled" in the landscape. Ray Lentner and his sons, Jerry and Henry, formed mini mountains along the northwest parking lot from the many cubic yards of topsoil that were excavated from the building site. These man-made mountains add to the Bavarian beauty of Bronner's.

Wally is especially appreciative of the combined efforts of wife Irene; daughter Carla; and managers Eddie Beyerlein, Anne Koehler, Doris Reda, and Jeanne Borcherding Braeutigam for their leadership in the relocation process.

The screen-printing business opened in October of 1976. The Christmas building opened its doors on June 8th, 1977, just in time for the annual Bavarian Festival. In addition to the one-acre (43,560 square feet) salesroom, the new building devoted an acre to warehouse and office space. Leota Hurford was the manager of the expansive salesroom. Additional storage space was rented in three off-site warehouses located a few blocks from Bronner's.

Bronner's ½-mile long Christmas Lane was developed alongside the new Christmas building. The delightful drive is spanned with decorative arches and dazzling displays, and is lit every evening.

The spacious parking lot at the new location at 25 Christmas Lane accommodated over 600 cars and recreational vehicles as well as 40 motorcoaches when built in 1976. (Lot expansions in 1991 and 1996 increased parking to a total of nearly 1,250 cars and 50 motorcoaches.) Holiday décor extends to the parking lot where gigantic, 4-foot, painted snowflakes cover various parking spaces. Each lamppost along Christmas Lane bears the 25 Christmas Lane address in one of over 75 languages.

Guests are welcomed in over 60 languages from a large sign in the entrance. "Thank you," "See you again," and "God bless you" in many languages send guests on their way at the exit.

The logo of BRONNER'S CHRISTmas WONDERLAND is a familiar one to many people who have seen it in newspapers and on outdoor advertising. Approximately 60 billboards may be seen along highways and interstate turnpikes in Michigan, Ohio, Indiana, Pennsylvania, and Missouri. The most distant is in Sebring on Interstate 75 near Ocala, Florida, just north of Disney World.

In 1976, William G. Milliken, governor of Michigan, recognized BRONNER'S CHRISTmas WONDERLAND as an attraction for guests throughout the USA, Canada, Mexico and other nations. The Embassy For Michigan Tourism Award plaque reads in part, "I hereby bestow this honor and its attendant privileges and responsibilities in recognition of outstanding and significant contributions to the Michigan tourist industry."

"EDUTAINER" STYLE SPEAKER - Wally Bronner annually presents 250 educational, motivational, and inspirational speeches to groups in convention halls, classrooms, churches, television and radio studios, and Bronner's program center. Wally narrated the video, "God's Miraculous Gift of Life," for a Canadian pro-life group.

Start of Relocation

Star of the West Milling Company manager, **DICK KRAFFT** (left), purchased Bronner's three properties at the corner of Main and Tuscola Streets. **RAO MANYAM** (center) was the consulting engineer, and **TOM SCHMIDT** (right) was the architect for the new buildings on the south end of town.

RON BRONNER Wally's cousin, was the general contractor.

THE LENTNER BROTHERS (Jerry and Henry) shaped Bronner's "mini-Alps" from the excavated soil from the building and parking lot sites.

Bronner's Screen Printing

Bronner's sign artist **FRANK FULCO** painted a rendering of the proposed new building for Bronner's Screen Printing.

Construction was completed in the spring of 1976.

The spacious production area accommodated the
54-FT. SCREEN-PRINTING PRODUCTION LINE.

Memtron Technologies

Manager **DON FISCHER** introduced a new name for Bronner's Screen Printing to better describe the varied product line of membrane switches. ("Mem" for membrane and "tron" for electronics)

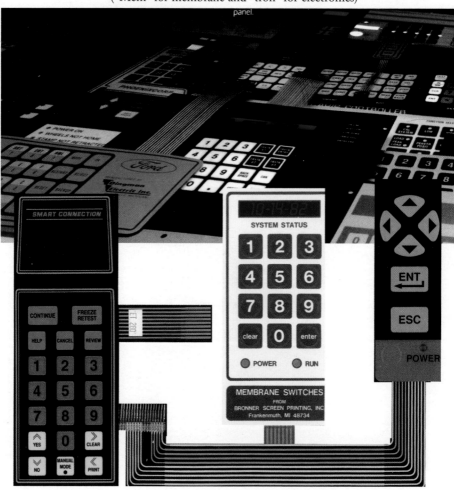

Photo montage of **MEMBRANE SWITCHES**.

Artistic Diversity

TRUCK LETTERING and **GRAPHICS** were a major part of the business.

DON FISCHER, manager of Bronner's Screen Printing, sculpted a **BARRY GOLDWATER** bust from plastic foam for Dow Industries.

Painting by **FRANK FULCO** on display in Bronner's salesroom.

93

25 Christmas Lane

IRENE and **WALLY** with building plans. The billboard at the building site informed the public about the proposed new building.

The **FIRST COMPONENT ON SITE WAS A BOILER.** A utility company deadline for hookup and use of natural gas was the reason for the premature placement.

The **AERIAL VIEW** shows the foundation and partial walls. The **BUILDING WAS DESIGNED TO LOOK LIKE MULTIPLE BUILDINGS.**

Opening Day June 8, 1977

BRONNER'S
CHRISTmas
WONDERLAND

Originated in 1945 By Wallace "Wally" Bronner

Relocated to this site in 1977

Wally and Irene Bronner and Family
Dedicate this Business
IN THANKFULNESS TO GOD
and in memory of Wally's parents,
HERMAN and ELLA BRONNER

Wally and Irene

Expressions including "Welcome,"
and "See You Again," in many
languages convey an
INTERNATIONAL ATMOSPHERE at
the all-new location at 25 Christmas
Lane.

Bronner's Road Signs

ABOUT 60 BILLBOARDS in numerous states inform travelers of Bronner's CHRISTmas Wonderland.

A FLORIDA BILLBOARD on I-75 invites travelers from 50 states and all Canadian provinces and territories.

Original parking lot accommodated 600 vehicles. During some peak days, vehicle license plates can be seen from more than 25 states and provinces.

25 Christmas Lane

Nearly **100 MULTILINGUAL ADDRESS PLAQUES** appear along 1/2-mile (.8 KM) Christmas Lane.

LITTER CONTAINERS are identified in many languages.

Visitors enjoy seeing **MILE** and **KILOMETER DISTANCES** to locations around the world. The bottom line shows that Bronner's south entrance is 55 steps away.

The **DEER-XING SIGN** indicates "regulatory" compliance!

Parking Space Galore

More and more visitors converge to the **ALL-NEW LOCATION AT 25 CHRISTMAS LANE**.

The record number of coaches arriving in one day is 53.

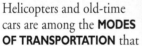

Helicopters and old-time cars are among the **MODES OF TRANSPORTATION** that can be seen in the parking lot, which is striped and decorated with 4-ft. snowflakes.

7 | Bronner's Doubles in Size

As guests enter Bronner's, they find the spacious salesroom alive with action, lights and color. Cheery staff members in attractive uniforms greet guests and offer assistance. Background music features selections most often heard during the yuletide season. Wally can often be seen sporting a red jacket with a sprig of holly on the lapel, green trousers, and red or green shoes.

Bronner's features over 500 different Nativity scenes, in sizes from one inch in height to life-size. Tiny scenes in wood or glass may be hung as tree ornaments. Other Nativity scenes are perfect for placing on the mantel or under the tree and include wood stables from Frankenmuth and some with moss or straw roofs crafted in Germany and Italy. Handcrafted sets from Peru, Russia, Nigeria, the Philippines, India, Mexico, and Bethlehem are among the offerings. Larger Nativities can be found in the stunning, resin Fontanini line and the 17-figure, fiberglass, life-size scene formed from Bronner's patented molds.

Guests are invited to feast their eyes on all sizes and kinds of artificial trees and trims in the mammoth tree and ornament section. Over 260 trees are tastefully trimmed and lighted by Bronner's tree decorating specialists. Classic tree themes include angels, religion, weddings, anniversaries, births, Victorian decor, Santa, snowmen, teddy bears, fruits and vegetables, and the great outdoors, as well as other designer trees. Garlands, lights, thousands of ornaments, and a variety of trims all in one location make for shopping ease. Decorations for the trees come from around the world, offering shoppers an awesome selection that includes exclusive Bronner designs not seen elsewhere.

Personalized ornaments originated at a staff Christmas party in the early years of the Bronner business. Wally hand-lettered ornaments for staff members' children as a special party gift. So many requests came in for personalized ornaments following the party that personalized ornaments were soon added to Bronner's line. Now Bronner's carries ornaments bearing about 150 stock names. Staff artists hand-letter about 100,000 ornaments yearly, inscribing special or unusual names and inscriptions such as birth, wedding, anniversary, or retirement dates. The artists have even been asked to letter marriage proposal messages on the ornaments!

The store offers ornaments with "Merry Christmas" in more than 70 languages. Thirty styles of international ornaments bear the nation's Christmas greeting on one side and a description of that nation's holiday customs and traditions on the reverse side.

Wally says, "When it comes to mass-producing glass ornaments, the United States has no equal. However, many people ask us for the handmade, traditional, nostalgic, European-looking variety. They're usually looking for the kind of antique decorations Grandma had on her tree or ornaments they remember from their youth - childhood treasures."

It is believed that a chemist in Lauscha, Germany, produced the first blown-glass Christmas tree ornaments in the middle of the 19th century. These first ornaments were blown from slender, glass tubes. The glass balls were hung from the trees by strings attached to corks plugged into their open end.

The 150th anniversary of glass tree ornament production was observed in Lauscha in July 1997. Wally participated in the celebration. He spoke in the city's church and also delivered a congratulatory message to the assembled glass industry workers at the festival pavilion.

In addition to the many USA-produced glass ornaments, Bronner's imports mouth-blown ornaments from Germany, Austria, Italy, Poland, the Czech and Slovak Republics, Romania, Hungary, Columbia, Mexico, the Ukraine, Russia, Egypt, and the Far East. Six thousand different styles of ornaments are available at Bronner's.

From the early years of business, particularly after the purchase of the Bavarian Corner in 1971, Bronner's has featured the renowned M.I. Hummel figurines by the W. Goebel Porzellanfabrik in Rödental, Germany. The M.I. Hummel figurines are created from the artwork of Sister Maria Innocentia Hummel, a Franciscan nun. Her work attracted the attention of executives at the Goebel factory, who obtained worldwide rights to transform the two-dimensional creations of M.I. Hummel into three-dimensional figurines. Because of their popularity as gifts and collectibles, Hummel figurines have been labeled "The World's Best-loved Children."

June Auernhammer, a Bronner staff member in the 1950s, suggested that the business start a collection that would include every Hummel figurine, thereby giving visitors to the store the opportunity to view and enjoy all of them. Bronner's growing private collection of over 1,000 Hummel figurines has proven popular in Frankenmuth, "Michigan's Little Bavaria," because of the German origin of the figurines first brought to the USA by members of the military who served in the European military theater in World War II. Bronner's is one of the largest Hummel dealers and has received various global awards including Goebel National Retailer of the Year.

Bronner's also has a private collection of over 1,700 Enesco Precious Moments figurines (based on the artwork of Sam Butcher), one of each figurine produced for the first 25 years of the collection (production started in 1978). Sam personally viewed the collection when he visited Bronner's Precious Moments Days as a special guest. Both collections are exhibited in Bronner's program center and may be viewed by the public.

Some of the early Christmas panels Wally designed for the City of Clare are also on display in Bronner's program center. Included in Bronner's program center collections is the first, near life-size Nativity scene that Wally produced for the Gera Dramatic Walther League display on the lawn of Frankenmuth's St. Lorenz School.

In addition to the above collections which are displayed in Bronner's program center (which seats about 200 people), the "World of Bronner's" presentation is shown daily free of charge. This 20-minute presentation premiered in June of 1984. It gives visitors a visual overview of the origins and growth of Bronner's through the years, and highlights the design and production of Bronner's worldwide selection of over 50,000 trims and gifts. The program evolved over the course of two years of planning and production by Todd Spence and the Bronner family. Todd Spence, owner of Spence & Associates, was the producer of the show which was originally produced as a 10-projector multi-image presentation. Music for the "World of Bronner's" was directed by Maestro Leo Najar, Director of the Saginaw Symphony, and recorded by the Saginaw Symphony and the Saginaw Choral Society in 1983 in St. Lorenz Lutheran Church where the accoustics were excellent for recording. Todd Spence has produced updates to the presentation through the years. In 2000, Todd converted the "World of Bronner's" to a digital DVD format. Over one million guests have viewed the presentation since it began.

The program center also serves as a museum, exhibiting more than 500 Nativity scenes from numerous countries and a collection of very special glass ornaments. The display includes a few favorite ornaments set aside from different five-year periods during Bronner's years in business. One, large, teardrop-shaped ornament bears a religious painting done for Wally by Italian artist Maria Louisa DeCarlini in the 1960s. Of special interest in the display are sketches of ornament designs drawn by members of Bronner's staff as they prepared the designs for forwarding to artists in Europe for production. Guests may also view an exhibit of progressive phases of glass ornament production.

December 22 & 23 are the annual dates for public, Christmas sing-alongs in Bronner's program center. Irene plays the old-fashioned pump organ and Wally and Bob Spletzer lead the caroling.

In 1985 it became apparent that even the new Bronner's building was not large enough to properly display the vast array of 50,000 trims and gifts. On peak days and weekends, Bronner's guests found themselves elbow to elbow with merchandise, staff, and other guests.

In the fall of 1985, a general staff meeting was held to generate ideas for building expansion. From 1985 to 1989, building ideas were collected in meetings and from the suggestion box. The Bronner family, as well as Bronner managers, supervisors, and assistant supervisors sorted through the suggestions and selected those which would be incorporated in the expansion. The architectural firm of Manyam and Associates was contacted in the fall of 1989 to put the plans on paper. It was a repeat performance for Rao Manyam, mechanical engineer; Tom Schmidt, architect in charge of the project; and Ron Bronner, general contractor. All three gentlemen masterminded the original Bronner construction at 25 Christmas Lane in 1977.

In December of 1989, construction for Bronner's expansion was underway with groundbreaking. In order to better serve a growing number of guests, Bronner's expanded its facilities in three phases during 1990 and 1991.

The first of the three phases converted approximately 5,000 square feet of warehouse space into additional salesroom area at a cost of approximately $300,000. This transformation was necessary in order to connect the new expansion on the north side of the building with the original 25 Christmas Lane salesroom.

The second phase was completed by the end of 1990 when Bronner's moved its shipping, maintenance, and ornament-lettering departments into an 18,000 square-foot building immediately north of Bronner's. Bronner's had leased the building for several years to Memtron Technologies, formerly Bronner Screen Printing. In 1980 Bronner Screen Printing incorporated as a separate entity, Memtron Technologies, managed by Don Fischer. In 1984, Don and Karen Fischer purchased the business and leased the building from Bronner's. During early 1991, Memtron moved to an all-new, impressive facility built on the north end of the city, allowing Bronner's to utilize the building space that Memtron had leased. An enclosed 375-ft. corridor connected the former Memtron building with the new addition. A small fleet of bicycles and motorized carts allowed the staff to travel quickly back and forth through the corridor.

Phase three was the construction of a 95,000 square-foot addition to BRONNER'S CHRISTmas WONDERLAND, with 22,000 square feet devoted to expanded salesroom area. The additional salesroom area provided much more "elbow room" for guests to shop and more room for merchandise displays. The expansion also included a second, four-lane, drive-through, canopy-covered entrance; a large lobby; lockers; additional checkout area; additional public restrooms; and a new snack area called "Season's Eatings," featuring light snacks and refreshments (including Christmas cookies all year). The remainder of the new space was utilized for behind-the-scenes warehousing, receiving, offices, and staff facilities.

With the completion of the three-phase building expansion in the summer of 1991, Bronner's equaled 5.5 acres (over 236,000 square feet or 4 football fields) of building space, with over 62,000 square feet (1-1/3 football fields) devoted to salesroom and display area for guests to enjoy. The total sales area was increased by more than 76 percent when the warehouse conversion and new construction were completed. Many new and expanded facilities added to guest and staff comfort and convenience. The cost of the entire project, which doubled the size of the original building, was approximately $6 million.

In keeping with German custom, a "Topping Party" for the building addition was held when the framework of the structure was roughed in. The builders placed a lighted tree on top of the roof, signaling that it was time for a party to be held.

Open houses for the new expansion were held for the staff and their families, media, business associates, and the Frankenmuth community. Governor John Engler was the keynote speaker at the business open house, visiting Bronner's with his wife Michelle, who cut the unique ribbon composed of decorative gift certificates for 20 local religious, charitable and civic groups.

Events and Exhibits

Events are free to all visitors.

The program center features a complete selection of more than **1,000 HUMMEL FIGURINES** ranging from 3 to 30 inches (7 to 70 centimeters).

Bronner personnel in **ALPINE-STYLE UNIFORMS** greet and meet visitors from around the world. (Left to right) Nancy Schneider, Betty Caswell, Wally, Lorene Bronner, Wayne Bronner, Doris Reda and Carla Bronner Spletzer.

The **NATIVITY SCENE COLLECTION** includes over 500 sets made in the arts and crafts styles of 70 nations.

GLASS ORNAMENT PRODUCERS from Lauscha, Germany, the cradle of the ornament industry, demonstrate glassblowing and decorating techniques at Bronner's.

PRECIOUS MOMENTS 20TH ANNIVERSARY
Care-A-Van visits Bronner's in 1998.

ARTIST SAM BUTCHER, designer of Precious Moments figurines, enjoys the figurine display. Thousands of collectors come for his appearances.

Exclusive Bronner ornament designs by **STAFF ARTIST CONNIE LARSEN** are transformed into tree ornaments in global glass studios. The designs have also been adapted for cross-stitch books.

At an Austrian studio, **WAYNE BRONNER, DORIS REDA** and **NANCY SCHNEIDER** inspect ornaments that are sold in Bronner's store, catalogs, and on the website.

Global Array of Trims

A program center exhibit features a representative **COLLECTION OF ORNAMENTS** produced in Europe and USA.

MARIA DE CARLINI, Italian artist, handpainted the 8-inch (20cm) JOY ornament.

Glass tree ornaments originated in 1847. In 1997, Wally was a guest speaker for the 150th anniversary in Lauscha. (Industrial glass production started in 1597.)

In 1989, at the time of the fall of the wall in Berlin, **WALLY** and **IRENE** hammered out remembrance segments.

Wally discovered the **FONTANINI** line of **ARTISTIC NATIVITY SCENE FIGURES** at a 1966 trade fair in Milano, Italy. Bronner's was the first to import the sets to the USA.

Irene Bronner (center) met **ROSANNA** and her husband **UGO FONTANINI** grandson of **EMANUELE, SR.** who founded the firm in 1908.

JIMMY THOMPSON, his wife **MYRA** and their daughter **MARTHA**, acquainted Irene and Wally with Caffco factories in the Philippines and China.

Screen Print Division Sold

In 1984 Irene and Wally sold Bronner's Screen Print Division and Memtron Technologies to **DON FISCHER** and his wife **KAREN**, shown with longtime legal advisor Robert Stroebel (center).

In 1990 Construction Starts to Double Size of Christmas Headquarters

The **FOUR-STORY BUILDING** added 100,000 sq. ft. (9,302 sq. m.).

Wally and team built displays.

A system of **ICE STORAGE TANKS** were installed for economical cooling.

BRONNER'S CHRISTmas WONDERLAND

[1991 Addition]

Dedicated with thankfulness to God

Most of the construction was completed for the 1991 peak season.

GOVERNOR JOHN and **MICHELLE ENGLER** dedicated the building in 1992. Maria Bronner Sutorik left, Wayne Bronner, Irene and Wally, Governor Engler and his wife Michelle.

On Epiphany, January 6, in Central Europe, some people dressed as wisemen make door-to-door visits to gather gifts for the needy. Above the door they inscribe **C✝M✝B**, placing a cross between each letter. Many interpret the letters to represent the legendary names of the Magi Caspar, Melchior, and Balthasar. In reality the letters originate from the Latin phrase, "Christus Mansem Benedicat" (Christ Bless This Home).

Space! Space! Space!

Christmas caroling in **PROGRAM CENTER** in 1991.

Christmas cookies are popular 361 days of the year. Clockwise from left: **KATHY ELWOOD, PAM ROLAND, GLADYS CUSTER, CATHY MAULE, EMMA MONTAGUE, JANET TIEDEMAN**.

SEASON'S EATINGS SNACK AREA accommodates 120 people.

GIGANTIC SALESROOM features wide aisles and well-stocked displays.

111

BRONNER'S PROGRAM CENTER IS POPULAR - The center is open 361 days of the year. Visitors can view Nativity scenes, 1,000 Hummel figurines, and all the Precious Moments figurines from the first 25 years of production. Also to be seen is a selection of glass ornaments from numerous countries. Over 500 depictions of the Nativity are displayed from over 50 global nations.

The center has scheduled video showings about Bronner's and its history and other scheduled presentations. Numerous clubs, schools and college classes visit annually. Never a charge!

MANY MOVIES CONTAIN PROPS FROM BRONNER'S - Hollywood and Canadian and other film studios have selected Bronner's as an ideal source for decorative props and scenes for Christmas and seasonal-themed productions. Naturally we are pleased that our staff and stock can be of help year-round.

The movie directors and props managers are likewise pleased to be able to browse through a variety of over 50,000 decorations that cover a wide range of subjects and eras.

BRONNER'S FLAVORFUL FAVORITES - That's the title of a well-received 3-ring notebook style cookbook which features over 400 recipes.

Bronner's 60th year and a suggestion triggered the action to produce a cookbook that contains over 400 favorite recipes submitted by many of Bronner's 500 staffers.

Missing from the book is what Wally Bronner makes best for meals...reservations!

EUROPEAN ALPINE SCENES - William "Tiny" Zehnder and Judy Zehnder Keller honored Wally by asking him to purchase "just the right" oil paintings and prints for the walls of the Bavarian Inn Restaurant and Bavarian Inn Lodge while he was on a buying trip.

8 | Bronner's Replica of the Silent Night Memorial Chapel

Another building dream that came true for Wally Bronner was the construction of the Silent Night Memorial Chapel. "Stille Nacht" ("Silent Night") is the most beloved and widely known Christmas hymn in the entire world. In fact, the hymn has been translated into more languages than any other sacred Christmas song. Pastor Joseph Mohr wrote the verses and teacher Franz Xaver Gruber composed the music for the inspiring hymn that was first sung on Christmas Eve in 1818 in St. Nicholas Church of Oberndorf, Austria. The music is peaceful and the words proclaim the Biblical Christmas message of the birth of Christ the Savior.

St. Nicholas Church was damaged by the annual high waters of the Salzach River that flow from the Alps in the Salzburg region. The church was rebuilt on higher ground, and the Silent Night Memorial Chapel was erected on a landscaped mound over the original altar site to commemorate the 100th anniversary of the carol. Construction was started in 1924 and the chapel was completed and consecrated on August 15, 1937.

In 1976, Wally Bronner made a visit to the Oberndorf Silent Night Memorial Chapel during a European buying trip. He was inspired with the idea of duplicating that chapel in Frankenmuth, providing permission would be granted by the Oberndorf community, located 10 miles north of Salzburg. A visit with Oberndorf City Manager Herbert Lämmermeyer brought encouraging results: approval would likely be granted if a formal request were made to the Bürgermeister (mayor) and city council of Oberndorf.

Annual business trips to European trade fairs during the late '70s and '80s provided opportunities for buyers Edna Martens, Leota Hurford, Doris Reda, and Nancy Schneider to visit the

Oberndorf chapel to detail measurements and special features of the structure. Irene Bronner, members of the Bronner family, and builder Ron Bronner also made visits to ensure authenticity.

During a 1989 buying trip to Europe, salesroom manager Leota Hurford, Wally Bronner, and Volker and Waltraud Wratschko (Wally's business friends from Austria), met with Mayor Dr. Raimund Traintinger at the Oberndorf City Hall. Wally made a formal request in the German language for permission to duplicate the chapel.

In November 1989, the City Government and Visitors' Bureau of Oberndorf granted official written approval for the Bronner family to replicate the original chapel in Frankenmuth, Michigan, providing these guidelines were observed: The replica should be constructed following as closely as possible the style of the original chapel building. The memorial chapel should be used for visitation and meditation and to tell the story of Silent Night. It should not be used for scheduled services or ceremonies. Bronner's should inform visitors to the chapel replica about the original Silent Night Chapel in Oberndorf. Original works of art should be simulated but not duplicated.

Ground was broken in the spring of 1992 for the replica in Frankenmuth. Ron Bronner, his son Matt, and team leader Ken Block took special interest in the project for on-time completion. That autumn Irene and Wally attended the World's Fair in Seville, Spain, and then visited Oberndorf to finalize arrangements for the chapel dedication. The chapel was completed for dedication on November 20, 1992. Former Mayor of Oberndorf Dr. Raimund Traintinger, his wife Ingebord, and their daughter Ingrid were special guests at the dedication ceremonies along with business friends Volker Wratschko and son Norbert from Austria. The chapel opened to the public a day later, November 21. The dedicatory plaque reads: "With special permission from the government and tourist association of Oberndorf, Austria, near Salzburg, this replica of Oberndorf's original Silent Night Memorial Chapel was erected in Frankenmuth, Michigan, in 1992 as a tribute to the Christmas hymn Stille Nacht (Silent Night), which was first sung in Oberndorf in 1818. This memorial is in thankfulness to God from Wally and Irene Bronner and family."

The octagonal-shaped 28' x 28' x 56' tall building is nestled in the rolling, landscaped mounds at the south end of Bronner's property. Outside the chapel, plaques with a verse of the hymn "Silent Night" in over 300 languages are displayed along a tranquil, lamppost-lined walkway featuring a "Silent Night" musical score arch and an inspiring, white, life-size Nativity. A walkway through the peaceful chapel interior allows visitors to view the chancel through a glass partition. Looking into the chancel area, guests can admire an altar bearing a replica of Oberndorf's hand-crocheted filet altar cloth (handstitched by Bronner staff member Doris Reda); a crucifix made in 1818 (presented to Bronner's by Theodore "Ted" Smithey); pews; and a Bronner-produced, majestic Nativity scene. A Christmas tree decorated in an early Austrian motif, garlands, a wreath with a guitar cradled in it, information about the hymn and its composers, and a reproduction of the original musical score are included in the chapel display. A large Advent wreath, star, and crown are suspended from the wooden ceiling. The Biblical account of the Christmas message (Luke 2: 1-19) is displayed in 33 languages. The central wooden door of the chapel bears an inscription that was carved by Bronner's staff artist, Connie Larsen, and features an angel design like that of Oberndorf's chapel. The message reads: "Friede den Menschen auf Erden die einer guten Willen sind." (Glory to God in the highest and peace to His people on earth.)

Beautiful stained-glass windows add to the serene atmosphere. The staff of BRONNER'S CHRISTmas WONDERLAND surprised the Bronner family by commissioning a local glass firm to produce the two stained-glass windows for the chapel as a Christmas gift in honor of the business' 50th year. One window portrays Mary, Joseph, and the infant Jesus. The other window depicts an angel appearing to the shepherds. Connie Larsen, a Bronner's staff artist, sketched the designs for the windows, which were skillfully crafted by Kathy Chesney of Kelley Glass in Saginaw. The Bronner family had hoped to have stained-glass windows produced for the chapel by the year 2000, but thanks to the generosity and kindness of the staff, the windows were in place five years ahead of schedule for the enjoyment of many.

Information about Bronner's replica, the original chapel in Oberndorf, and the community of Oberndorf is on display within the chapel. "Silent Night" may be heard inside the chapel and wafting over the chapel grounds. The chapel, topped by a brilliant gold star, is fully illuminated at night. This inspirational landmark awaits guests at the south entrance to the City of Frankenmuth. Guests from over 100 nations annually sign the guest register. Every December 24 at 3 p.m., guests fill the chapel as Wally retells the story of "Silent Night" and leads the singing of "Stille Nacht" in German and in English to the accompaniment of a guitarist.

While gathering "Silent Night" in various versions of the world, Irene and Wally were pleased to receive the musical score in Arabic. They were puzzled because the Arabic arrangement seemingly had a different melody. Eventually, Wally discovered that Arabic music reads from right to left. It was the real "Silent Night" melody after all!

In the spring of 1999, Wally and Irene were invited to tour the remodeled Silent Night Museum in Fügen, Tyrol province, Austria. Organ builder Carl Mauracher had brought "Stille Nacht" to his hometown of Fügen (east of Innsbruck) in the spring of 1819. The Strasser and Rainer folk singers from Fügen included the song in their concerts, helping to spread the popularity of the carol in Europe. In 1839 the Rainers brought "Silent Night" to the USA when they sang it in front of Wall Street's Trinity Church in New York City. The Bronner family made a contribution toward the restoration of the Rainer family tombstone in the Fügen church cemetery.

At the 1999 Joseph Mohr Silent Night Symposium in Wagrain, Austria, the government of Austria expressed special appreciation to Wally and Irene Bronner and family. Landeshauptmann (Governor) Dr. Franz Shausberger, governor of the state of Salzburg (one of Austria's nine states), presented Wally with a silver medallion of honor for "research, art and culture, and religion" in appreciation for deeds and activities that help the government of Salzburg spread the joyous history of "Stille Nacht" and its significance for Christianity throughout the world.

Austrian officials who have made visits to Bronner's chapel include Dr. Raimund Traintinger and Andreas Kinzel, former Oberndorf mayors; Dr. Ottmar Kundrath, long-time secretary of the Silent Night Association; and Peter Swartz, consul of Austria.

An excerpt from a letter dated February 8, 2005 from Landeshauptfrau Gabi Burgstaller (Governor of the state of Salzburg, Austria) states: "It is a great honour for our country that not only the peacemaking spirit of the world famous song, 'Silent Night' from Oberndorf near Salzburg, but also the Silent Night Chapel as a small part of Austria are presented in your CHRISTmas Wonderland in such dignified manner to millions of guests coming from the USA, from Canada, and from the whole world."

THE STORY OF SILENT NIGHT, HOLY NIGHT -
When the replica of the Oberndorf, Austria Silent Night Memorial Chapel was completed on a tract at Bronner's CHRISTmas Wonderland, many asked questions about the world's favorite Christmas carol. The decision was made to produce an English language video to relate the carol's history, information about the composers, the reason for the carol, the original memorial chapel and the replica in Frankenmuth, Michigan.

Replica of Silent Night Memorial Chapel

The replica of this original chapel in Oberndorf/Salzburg Austria was constructed as an expression of thankfulness to God for blessings to the Bronner family.

Builder **RON BRONNER** and Irene and Wally travel to Austria to view the Silent Night Memorial Chapel.

Irene and Wally discuss plans for the Silent Night Memorial Chapel replica with **MAYOR ANDREAS KINZL** and former **MAYOR DR. RAIMUND TRAINTINGER** of Oberndorf near Salzburg, Austria.

Construction began in the spring of 1992 on the Bronner property after **PERMISSION WAS RECEIVED FROM THE CITY GOVERNMENT OF OBERNDORF, AUSTRIA.**

KEN BLOCK was project supervisor.

DALE "MUNCHY" MUEHLFELD places the star on the cupola. The star was crafted by **JEROLD SCHREINER**.

DORIS REDA hand crocheted a filet altar cloth duplicate of the Oberndorf chapel altar cloth, which reads "Stille Nacht, Heilige Nacht." **DENNIS PFUND** crafted the replica star.

CONNIE LARSEN hand carved the inscription on the chapel's wooden door. She also rendered the artwork for the stained-glass windows that were crafted by **KATHY CHESNEY** of Kelley Glass in Saginaw, Michigan. The **STAINED-GLASS WINDOWS WERE A GIFT** to the Bronner family from their employees at the 1994 Christmas party.

"Stille Nacht" ("Silent Night") composed by **JOSEF MOHR** and **FRANZ GRUBER**, is the world's favorite Christmas carol.

WITH SPECIAL PERMISSION
FROM THE GOVERNMENT AND TOURIST ASSOCIATION
OF OBERNDORF, AUSTRIA, NEAR SALZBURG,
THIS REPLICA OF OBERNDORF'S ORIGINAL

Silent Night Memorial Chapel

WAS ERECTED IN FRANKENMUTH, MICHIGAN, IN 1992
AS A TRIBUTE TO THE CHRISTMAS HYMN
Stille Nacht (Silent Night)
WHICH WAS FIRST SUNG IN OBERNDORF IN 1818

THIS MEMORIAL IS IN THANKFULNESS TO GOD
FROM WALLY AND IRENE BRONNER AND FAMILY

THE CHAPEL IS A MEMORIAL
AND IS NOT INTENDED
FOR SERVICES OR CEREMONIES

KAREN HOFFMAN prepares documentation of Wally's speech given at the University of Salzburg for the 175th anniversary of the carol "Silent Night."

Plaques with one verse of the carol in **OVER 300 LANGUAGES** surround the chapel.

Silent Night Chapel Dedication November 20, 1992

Salzburg, Austria, newspaper **SALZBURGER NACHRICHTEN** Nov. 14, 1992 reads "Silent Night Chapel of Oberndorf duplicated in USA."

VOLKER WRATSCHKO, Austrian business associate, and **OBERNDORF'S MAYOR TRAINTINGER** at the dedication celebration.

Wally Bronner was a presenter in Oberndorf near Salzburg, Austria, for the **SILENT NIGHT ASSOCIATION**, annual meeting. Among attendees were Oberndorf's Mayor **PETER SCHROEDER,** Governor of the state of Salzburg **GABI BURGSTALLER**, Treasurer **ANDREAS KINZL**, President Konsul **BERTL EMBERGER**.

During the 1999 Josef Mohr Symposium in Wagrain Austria, **FRANZ SCHAUSBERGER**, governor of the state of Salzburg, presented Wally with the silver medal of "Science, Art and Religion."

The Bronner family welcomed five Austrian guests, area dignitaries, and citizens of Frankenmuth for the chapel dedication on November 20, 1992. Top left, **VOLKER WRATSCHKO**; top right, **NORBERT WRATSCHKO**; third row, **MAYOR TRAINTINGER** with wife **INGE** and daughter **INGRID**.

Grandsons **GARRETT** and **DIETRICH BRONNER** presented a message in German at the event.

The memorial chapel is on a landscaped plot at the southern edge of Bronner's CHRISTmas Wonderland. Annually, visitors from over 100 nations enter their names in the chapel guest register.

"Stille Nacht, Heilige Nacht"

Silent Night
Memorial
Chapel

9 | Catalog and Website Shopping

In 1989 under the direction of Wayne Bronner, Wally and Irene's son, the business developed a catalog, "Bronner's Christmas Favorites," for in-store distribution. In 1993 Bronner's began mailing the catalog to thousands of homes across the United States and around the world. Each year, the catalog business grew and the circulation increased. In 2005, the catalog's circulation reached 3,000,000 copies. From exclusive ornaments to heirloom Nativities, "Bronner's Christmas Favorites" offers a multitude of ideas for home decorating and holiday gift giving and is popular with Christmas enthusiasts in the USA, Canada and around the world.

Bronner's established its website at www.bronners.com in September of 1996. The site offers a wealth of information about the store, ornaments and decorations, special events, collectibles, decorations for cities and shopping centers, Bronner's Silent Night Chapel, fun facts and tips, online shopping, and Frankenmuth links. Bronner's catalog and website are increasingly important avenues for offering and distributing Christmas decor. Orders are received from around the world 24 hours a day throughout the year.

From a total staff of over 500 during the peak season, over 100 are involved in the catalog and internet operation. Included are three dozen operators in the call center where orders are taken seven days per week, with the rest involved in picking, packing and personalizing operations. The Bronner team prides itself on prompt and accurate order fulfillment.

www.bronners.com
...worldwide address!

...THOUSANDS OF ITEMS AVAILBLE ONLINE 24/7, 365 DAYS A YEAR.

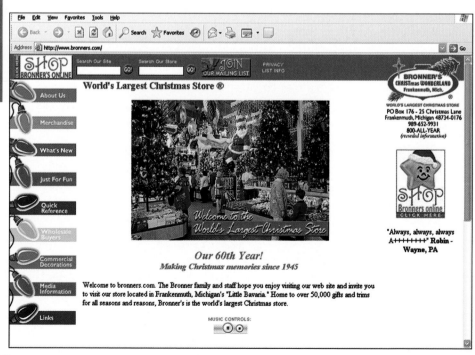

3 Million Catalogs Mailed Annually

The **RETAIL CATALOG**, started in 1989, features exclusive glass ornaments, heirloom Nativities, decorations, and gift items. The **WHOLESALE CATALOG** was started in 1973.

GIFT CARDS were introduced in 2003, replacing paper gift certificates.

BRONNER'S SCHEDULE OF EVENTS - An annual brochure and www.bronners.com keep Bronner's guests informed of special events such as artist appearances and promotions.

ORNAMENT LEGENDS, SYMBOLS & TRADITIONS - The Bronner team researched, edited, and published this book to share 75 legends, symbols and traditions with Christmas ornament enthusiasts.

BRONNER-DESIGNED ORNAMENTS - Since the mid 1960s, Bronner's has designed ornaments in religious, traditional, and toyland themes. In the 1970s, Bronner's began supplying custom ornaments to businesses, schools, churches, and clubs for use as fund-raisers, souvenirs, gifts, commemoratives, and promotions.

DEPARTMENT 56 COLLECTIBLES - The village scenes are displayed in Bronner's salesroom and visited by collectors from nearby and faraway.

From time to time Bronner's exclusive Dept. 56 accessories are offered - such as a car, bench and a building that has the character of Bronner's original Tannenbaum Shop.

PHOTOS WITH SANTA AND THE EASTER BUNNY - The costumed favorites are pleased to pose at no charge for those that bring their own cameras. Bronner's visual department provides impressive settings and backgrounds for the thousands of tots that visit seasonally.

Santa's red phone hot-line is available throughout the year at Bronner's store for his friends to listen to a message from him.

10 More Expansions 1996, 2000, 2001, 2003, 2004 & 2005

BRONNER'S CHRISTmas WONDERLAND celebrated its 55th anniversary in 2000 to the theme of expansion. In the fall of 1999, the shipping department was literally bulging at the seams due to increased in-store, catalog, commercial, and internet sales. A three-phase expansion was implemented to address the need for more space. Phase one, a 37,000-square-foot, two-story addition to BRONNER'S CHRISTmas WONDERLAND'S shipping department was completed just in time for the busy, fall 2000 shopping season. (The shipping department moved into the expansion in mid-September.) The addition brought 24 new packing stations, added a second story for stocking catalog inventory, and provided a spacious, new room for Bronner's personalized ornament painters, along with a new staff lounge and restrooms. The total cost of phase one was 2 million dollars.

In January of 2002, Bronner's purchased a warehouse on Heinlein Strasse (across the street from Bronner's) where they had previously rented some space. This 22,000-square-foot building provided additional storage space needed for the growing business.

Phase two consisted of an 80,000-square-foot expansion of Bronner's retail store, including additional space for Bronner's salesroom, customer service, and receiving departments. Three additional truckwells, stockroom, offices, and conference rooms were also completed in the expansion. Groundbreaking took place in spring 2001; the expansion opened in May 2002. The addition met the goals of having wider aisles to accommodate guests and shopping carts, greater space to display more of most every item offered for sale, a larger receiving area and additional stockroom and offices.

Bicycles and motorized carts are used to travel and move product behind the scenes. (Wally also rides his blue, one-speed, hand-brake bike decorated with a red bow and equipped with a horn. He can often be heard whistling "Rudolph, the Red-nosed Reindeer" and "Jingle Bells" as he rides along, accentuating the melodies with an occasional toot of the bike horn.)

To provide for all this growth, the third phase expanded the parking area to accommodate a total of 1,250 vehicles and 50 motorcoaches.

With all phases complete, the area "under the roof" is 320,000 square feet. An additional 48,000 square feet off-site brings Bronner's total to over 1/3 million square feet (6.4 football fields or 8.45 acres). Phase two was completed at a cost of 6 million dollars while phase three cost $500,000.

The dedication plaque on the newest addition reads:
BRONNER'S CHRISTmas WONDERLAND
2002 ADDITION DEDICATED WITH
THANKFULNESS TO GOD.

The 2001 expansion project was the result of an amazing combination of concepts, plans, and construction that met specific needs of the growing business. All members of the second generation met often to report their views and findings regarding specific assignments.

- Carla was responsible for evaluating the needs of customer service, checkout, and offices.
- Lorene's goal was to provide a generous and functional sales area with ample room for stock for easy shopping and checkout.
- Maria was concerned with making the addition as beneficial to onsite promotional events as possible.
- Chris built a model addition and provided some sketches of the addition to allow planners to better visualize the structure and assist his team in display building.
- Bob oversaw all facets of the construction to assure the new structure would meet current needs as well as provide for

future expansion.

- Wayne held the reigns on the overall monetary commitment to assure wise investment to serve current needs and anticipated growth in the next 5 to 10 years.
- Irene shared her enthusiasm and optimism, encouraging the planners to build large enough to provide for expansion as the need arises.
- Wally enjoyed observing the family and team leaders roll up their sleeves as they worked diligently to finish the expansion and open the area section by section. His experience from prior building expansion proved resourceful.

Long-time managers Anne Koehler, Mike Laux, and Dennis Pfund also had considerable input into various facets of the expansion. Their advice was based on experience gained from previous additions.

Dan Walter, hometown architect, was the master mind who provided us with plans for the most valuable use of each square foot of building.

Both Irene and Wally, at age 75, appreciated the unified and visionary planning by the second generation (age 50 and under). Their plans projected the potential of the third generation (some in their early 20s) becoming active in the business. A phrase that conveys applicable sentiments is that the family that prays together, plays together, plans together, and works together will stay together.

Ron Bronner Construction has built all the Christmas Wonderland expansions. (Ron and Wally are cousins; their grandfather was the first Bronner to enter the building trade.) Ron's son Matt is active in the construction business, and his children will probably comprise the fifth generation of Bronner builders in the USA.

During the early months of 2002, the interior rapidly began to resemble the "dreamed of" enlargement that would make the sales area 50 percent larger.

Busy bodies were everywhere – hammering, painting, constructing fixtures, carpeting, arranging displays, and stocking merchandise. Portions of the new area were in use by the public in mid-March. Work continued in April and was totally completed in May.

May 29, 2002, was the official opening date. Five hundred guests from the area business community were in attendance. Lt. Governor Dick Posthumus gave the dedicatory address.

All of the Bronner staff and their spouses had an opportunity to relax and inspect the expansion on the evening of May 30, 2002.

Additional landscaping and exterior displays were added. The prayer cross, a present from the staff to the Bronner family, was erected in the newly landscaped area just west of the addition. The solemn message in remembrance of September 11, 2001, reads: "Pray for world peace, faith, strength, comfort, love, and help."

Truly we are thankful to God that throughout 2002 guests came from near and far, stayed longer, and bought more. They enjoyed the spacious area, wider aisles, shopping carts, and seating areas.

The new, enlarged west checkout area and customer service area were ideal. Noticing that the south checkout area was overcrowded, the family decided to double and remodel that space immediately after the 2002 season ended.

The same team of builders, along with some members of the Bronner team, tackled the expansion of the south checkout area the first week of January. A completion date of early spring was set.

The expanded area accommodates additional automatic entry doors, a seating area with TV, more checkout space, shopping bags, baskets and carts, and an area for Santa to greet his visitors from the day after Thanksgiving through December 24.

Another remodeling was completed in spring of 2005. 2,100 sq. ft. of warehouse space was converted into additional salesroom area. Many merchandise displayers were added. Through the years the versatile Bronner team has designed and constructed numerous departmental displays. The prime goal of every change is to do what is best for the guest.

1996 Parking Lot Expansion

Longtime staff members **WAYNE BRONNER**, **BOB SPLETZER**, **MIKE LAUX**, and **DENNIS PFUND** provided expertise.

Evergreen trees were nestled in rock beds to beautify traffic islands.

Christmas Lane is illuminated every evening.

Expansion 2000

The 37,000-sq.-ft. (3,442 sq. meters), **TWO-STORY EXPANSION** (solid grey area in the sketch) depicts the shape of the two-story warehouse and shipping department addition.

MORE EXPANSIONS

WALLY BRONNER, WAYNE BRONNER and **BOB SPLETZER.**

TOM ERDMAN, Nuechterlein Electric; **RICK RUMMEL**, Trane Corp.; **MAC RODRIGUEZ** and **BOB BIERMAN**, Wm. Bronner & Son Contractors; **JERRY MOORE**, Remer Plumbing and Heating.

Grandson **DIETRICH BRONNER** inspects the expansive roof.

When the roof was completed... there was **CAUSE TO PAUSE AND PARTY. CARLA BRONNER SPLETZER**; **ANNE BRONNER**, Wm. Bronner and Son Contractors; **DENNIS PFUND**; **MIKE LAUX**; **FRED PARRENT**, Nuechterlein Electric; **DAN WALTER**, architect; **MEL VOLZ**, Nuechterlein Electric; **BOB SPLETZER**; **RON BRONNER**, Wm. Bronner and Son Contractors.

Construction specialists (back row) **JUDY MIATZ**, McMillan Associates; **DAN WALTER**, architect; **BOB SPLETZER**; **ED BARRY**, McMillan Associates; **TOM ERDMAN**, Nuechterlein Electric.
(front row) **BRANDEN RIEBENACK**, McMillan Associates; **KENNY BLOCK**, project manager with Wm. Bronner and Son Contractor

HOPES AND DREAMS of added storage space were fulfilled with spacious shelving … red and green, of course.

The Bronner Team "On the Ball"

The personalized ornament-lettering team has personalized hundreds of thousands of ornaments, including many for well-known personalities. Longtime Bronner personalized ornament artist **ARLINE WENZEL** with movie star **VAN JOHNSON**.

The personalized lettering artists enjoy their expanded facilities. (l to r clockwise) **VERNA DUBKE, BARB STEWART, DEANNE WEBER, AMY PEDDIE, SUELLEN VESPERMAN, CONNIE SCHLUCKEBIER, COLLEEN BATES, SARAH HARRINGTON, GAIL EADS, SUE KERN, GINGER DON, BILL BRINKER, GRETCHEN CONNORS,** and **LINDA BARRERA.**

Expanding Again...2002

80,000 sq. ft. (7,442 sq. m.) Approximately 2 acres.

CHRISTOPHER SUTORIK provided the artistic rendering of the proposed addition.

Months of planning proceeded groundbreaking. (l to r clockwise) **DENNIS PFUND, MARIA SUTORIK, MIKE LAUX, IRENE BRONNER, WAYNE** and **LORENE BRONNER, GARRETT BRONNER** (standing), **DIETRICH BRONNER, WALLY, CHRIS SUTORIK, ANNE KOEHLER, CINDY BAXTER, BOB** and **CARLA SPLETZER.**

A multitude of **TRADESPEOPLE COORDINATED THEIR SKILLS** to complete the building as scheduled.

METAL ROOFING STRIPS up to 150 ft. in length were roll-formed at the job site.

Every addition included the **TRADITIONAL TREE-TOPPING PARTY** where the client provides snacks and beverages for the builders as a gesture of appreciation.

EUROPEAN-TYPE BELLCOTS add décor to the roofline.

Who? What? When? Where?

Merchandise Manager **ANNE KOEHLER** explains the who, what, when, and where of the newest addition.

OUR TEAM OF SKILLED CARPENTERS designed and constructed all of the salesroom display units.

Ready!

BRONNER'S
CHRISTmas
WONDERLAND

2002 Addition

Dedicated with
thankfulness to God

The **GIGANTIC BRONNER'S LOGO** also functions as a unique air intake for the new structure.

Newspaper photographer **STEVE JESSMORE** and display consultant **KEVIN MAURER** with **WALLY**. Steve photographed Wally on his bike. Bicycles provide a fast behind-the-scenes method of transportation for the staff. A Wally-on-bike photo appears in the "Michigan 24/7" photo book by DK Publishing, 2004.

Grandsons **GARRETT BRONNER, PAUL**, **GREG**, and **RYAN SPLETZER** enjoy the added elbow room.

141

Dedication - May 29, 2002

MORE EXPANSIONS

MICHIGAN'S LT. GOV. DICK POSTHUMUS (with Wally and Irene) spoke a dedicatory message during the expansion open house on May 29, 2002.

The **BRONNER STAFF** presented the cross/plaque to the Bronner family at the 2002 Christmas party.

The **BRONNER FAMILY** at the dedication of the 2002 expansion – (l to r) Carla and Bob Spletzer; Lorene and Wayne Bronner; Wally and Irene; Paul, Greg and Ryan Spletzer; Garrett and Dietrich Bronner; Maria and Chris Sutorik.

BRONNER'S BILLBOARDS advertised the large expansion.

Focus on Freedoms

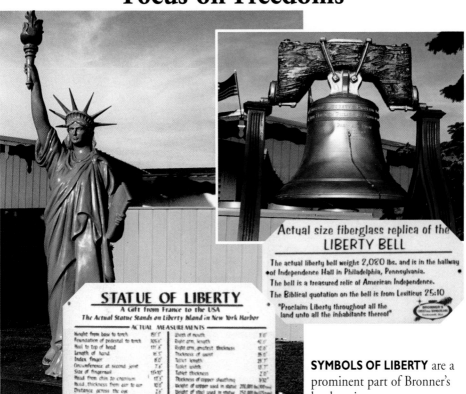

STATUE OF LIBERTY
A Gift from France to the USA
The Actual Statue Stands on Liberty Island in New York Harbor

ACTUAL MEASUREMENTS

The 8-5" Fiberglass Model is 5.6% of actual size

Actual size fiberglass replica of the LIBERTY BELL

The actual liberty bell weighs 2,080 lbs. and is in the hallway of Independence Hall in Philadelphia, Pennsylvania.
The bell is a treasured relic of American Independence.
The Biblical quotation on the bell is from Leviticus 25:10
"Proclaim Liberty throughout all the land unto all the inhabitants thereof"

SYMBOLS OF LIBERTY are a prominent part of Bronner's landscaping.

JAY BRANDOW of WNEM-TV5 interviewed **WALLY** and **BOB HEFT**, designer of the United State's current 50-star flag in use since 1960.

143

International Accents

FLAGS FROM 80 NATIONS welcome guests from around the world.

Cheers!

WAYNE BRONNER next to a currency display that features one, low-denomination monetary note from every nation in the world.

Bronner's includes an **INSPIRATIONAL DEVOTIONAL TRACT**
relative to the season in over-the-counter purchases,
correspondence, and shipping cartons. (1 million annually)

Everybody Loves A Parade!

Bronner's annual, themed parade float serves multiple purposes: it appears in Frankenmuth's Bavarian Festival Parade and Children's Parade, and also remains on display at Bronner's for photo opportunities and to represent float materials available at Bronner's.

1990 – World Peace

MORE EXPANSIONS

1995 - Frankenmuth's 150th Anniversary

2001 – "Sound of Music"

1993 - 175th Anniversary of "Silent Night" Christmas carol

1992 – 500th Anniversary of discovery of America

1999 - Generations of CHRISTmas Memories

2000 – Y2K and Bronner's 55th Anniversary

2004 - Tribute to the 100th Anniversary of Frankenmuth volunteer firefighters

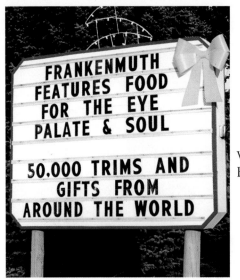

Signs Announce Events and Slogans

Various timely messages are conveyed on Bronner's changeable copy signs.

Colorful displays symbolize **EASTER** … the season that completes the CHRISTmas story. Decorating with eggs is a popular European custom.

CHRIST
OUR VICTORIOUS
KING

Displays and processions featuring Christian symbols formed with eggs are popular European Easter traditions.

Ornaments Galore

Many, exclusive Bronner designs are included in over
6,000 STYLES OF ORNAMENTS offered at Bronner's.

BRONNER'S CHRISTmas WONDERLAND
Frankenmuth, Mich.
www.bronners.com

Expanding To Serve You Better

Completion Summer of 2003

South Entrance Expanded

Wm. Bronner & Son	Dan Walter	MacMillan Associates	Nuechterlein Electric	Remer Plumbing & Heating	Lentner & Sons Excavating
General Contractors	Architect	Consulting Engineers			
Winninger Fire Protection	Trane Air Conditioning Systems			Johnson Controls	Stange Painting and Decorating

4,000-sq. ft. expansion.

The salesroom staff enjoyed making snowballs prior to installation of the roof.
(l to r) **KAREN GRAHAM**, **NANCY RUMMEL**, **SANDI MARTIN** and **DOROTHY BENMARK**.

Opening of Expanded South Entrance

The Bronner family hosted a thank-you celebration for the staff.

CARLA BRONNER SPLETZER and **BOB SPLETZER** with sons **GREG** and **RYAN**, **CHRIS SUTORIK** and **MARIA BRONNER SUTORIK, IRENE BRONNER, WAYNE BRONNER, DIETRICH BRONNER, PAUL SPLETZER, LORENE BRONNER, WALLY BRONNER.**

CHEF JOHN ZEHNDER (far left with hat) and Zehnder's Restaurant's catering team prepared the delicacies for the open house.

151

Year-Round Warehouses

Year-round warehouses provide storage area the size of a football field.

MIKE LAUX at CHRISTmas Wonderland warehouse located across the street from the main buildings.

Bronner's leases additional space on nearby List Street.

Over 2 Million Guests Annually

The Bronner family is most thankful for the increasing number of daily guests, averaging 2 million per year, who enjoy shopping at the World's Largest Christmas Store. The combined talent of the peak-time **STAFF OF OVER 500** truly is a blessing.

Bronner's has **900 SHOPPING CARTS** and **3,200 BASKETS**

2,500 Bronner shopping bags

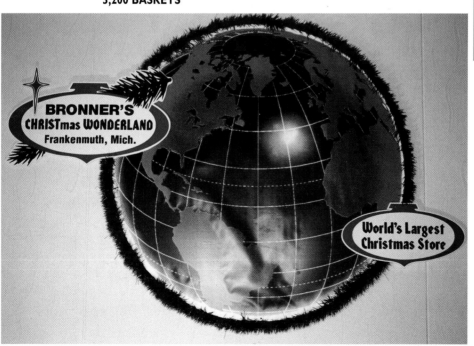

Guests from over **120 NATIONS** visit annually.

SQUARE FEET OR SQUARE METERS - Whichever measure is most recognizable conveys the size of Bronner's area under roof: 320,000 sq. ft.; 29,729 sq. m.; 7.35 acres; 3 hectares; or 5.5 football fields.

SNOWFLAKES YEAR ROUND - Four-foot snowflake designs can be seen on the asphalt surface as guide lines for Bronner's parking lot.

Simulated snowflakes fall for two minutes every 30 minutes on the hour and half hour in a portion of Bronner's west entrance lobby, generally from July 1 until Dec. 31. The mini snow flurries excite the children and are a favorite for photos and videos.

GLOBAL TELEVISION COVERAGE - Networks from every continent have aired coverage about Bronner's CHRISTmas Wonderland. Those nations include England, Scotland, Ireland, Lithuania, Germany, Austria, New Zealand, Brazil, Canada, Mexico and our own USA.

CHRISTMAS LANE - When the need arose for Bronner's to add parking spaces on the west side of the property, Dave Van Hine of the State of Michigan Transportation Department provided designs for a four-lane entrance and double-lane drive that serve a 1,000-plus vehicle parking area.

PLANNING REFERENCE: PAST, PRESENT, FUTURE - Bronner's 3-ring green cover notebook has 510 entries dating back to October 26, 1971. The management has kept notes concerning planning sessions, suggestions and ideas from staff and guests to be incorporated in various phases of building expansion projects.

The PAST and PRESENT phases are completed. The book has some entries for the FUTURE and many blank pages to add more.

11 | The Bronner Family

Wally Bronner, originator of BRONNER'S CHRISTmas WONDERLAND, is often in the store seven days a week unless he is on a buying trip or giving a speech locally, nationally, or internationally.

The Bronners have been blessed with four children. Each of Wally and Irene's two sons and two daughters started helping in the family business as children. Very early work experiences included assembling boxes for checkout, packaging candy, running errands, and unpacking and pricing merchandise. During high school, their jobs included painting signboards and completing screen-printing jobs, clerical work, salesroom, and checkout duties.

Eldest son Wayne joined the family business in 1983 as an assistant general manager and treasurer of the corporation. Wayne's wife Lorene also joined the staff in the same year as a salesroom manager. Wayne and Lorene's two sons, Dietrich and Garrett, began working at the business during their elementary school years.

Daughter Carla, married to Bob Spletzer, started full-time in the office in 1976 and began serving as an assistant general manager and corporate secretary in 1981. Bob joined the business in 1988 as Bronner's human resources and building manager. Carla and Bob have three sons: Ryan, Paul, and Greg.

Son Randall is an electrical engineer residing in Arizona.

Daughter Maria, married to Christopher Sutorik, joined the family business full-time in 1989 as marketing manager and assistant secretary for the corporation. Christopher became Bronner's visual merchandising manager in 1995. He currently serves as visual/internet merchandising manager.

All the children and their spouses had work experience in varied and important vocations prior to joining the growing family business.

In January of 1998, Wally and Irene announced the transfer of leadership to the second generation. Wayne was named president and chief executive officer, and Carla and Maria were named vice-presidents. Both Wally and Irene continue to be very active in the business and serve on the board, with Wally serving as board chairman.

As grandparents, Wally and Irene are very thrilled to have experienced the involvement of grandsons Dietrich and Garrett (children of Wayne and Lorene) assisting part-time in the business during their college years. An additional joy is knowing that three more grandsons – Ryan, Paul, and Greg (sons of Carla and Bob) – are expressing interest in being active in the tri-generation business.

The year 2001 was time to pause for a "golden touch." All the Bronner staff gathered on the evening of May 31 for a staff-sponsored tribute to Wally and Irene in recognition of a special blessing from the Lord, 50 years of marriage.

The second generation also realized their goal of extensive video coverage regarding Wally's 56 years of business experience. A DVD presentation of the Wally Bronner story entitled "A Decorative Life: the Wally Bronner Story" is shown in Bronner's program center on a scheduled basis.

THE SECOND GENERATION - The Bronner family's second generation worked in various positions prior to coming to the family business. These experiences prepared them to lead the growing CHRISTmas Wonderland.

Son Wayne served on the staff of the Michigan Department of Wildlife. His wife Lorene worked for the Lansing Department of Light and Water, National Forest Service, and a newspaper office.

Daughter Carla served in the department for off-campus education at Central Michigan University. Her husband Bob was employed as a teacher, painter, realtor, musician, and restaurant owner.

Daughter Maria served in an advertising agency. Her husband, Christopher, with a mechanical engineering and art background, worked for major industries, a department store, and a newspaper.

Parents Irene and Wally feel blessed to have such talents in the family.

Still-Active Originators Transfer
Leadership to Second Generation

Wayne Bronner
President & CEO
Joined 1983

Carla Bronner Spletzer
Vice President
Joined 1976

Maria Bronner Sutorik
Vice President
Joined 1989

Lorene S. Bronner
Salesroom Manager
Joined 1983

Bob Spletzer
HR & Building Manager
Joined 1988

Christopher Sutorik
Visual Display Manager
Joined 1995

Bronner Family Yesteryear and Now

The Bronner family 1967: Wally and Irene, children (l-r) Maria, Randy, Wayne, and Carla.

The Bronner family 2001:
Front row: Lorene S. Bronner, Maria Bronner Sutorik, Carla Bronner Spletzer, Greg Spletzer, Paul Spletzer. Middle row: Wayne Bronner, Christopher Sutorik, Bob Spletzer, Ryan Spletzer, Garrett Bronner. Back row: Wally and Irene, Randy Bronner, Dietrich Bronner.

Golden Wedding Anniversary

June 23, 2001

Son **RANDY BRONNER** is an electrical engineer and photographer residing in Fountain Hills, Arizona.

"**A DECORATIVE LIFE: THE WALLY BRONNER STORY**" produced by Todd Spence (right), assisted by Kevin Copus (center).

Top to bottom - "Bronner's CHRISTmas Wonderland" 1989, "**THE WALLY BRONNER STORY**" 2002, "Christmas Dreams Come True at Bronner's" video and DVD 2002 and "Silent Night" video 1994.

159

DAYS THAT END IN "Y" - "My hobby of signs, displays, and decorations developed into a full-time business, and I never went to work," Wally said. "Since I never went to work, I don't have to think of retirement, and I'll continue the hobby, God-willing, but only on days that end in 'y.'"

WALLY AND IRENE AND FAMILY ARE GRATEFUL FOR REFERENCE TO BRONNER NAME - Some buildings, scholarships, awards and events give reference to the name Bronner.

A family even selected Bronner as their son's name - because he was born on Christmas day.

"Looks like a mini Bronner's" is a comment heard by some people that love decorations at their homes or business.

ORIGIN OF BRONNER'S MOTTO - While Wally was international president of the Walther League, an organization of young Lutherans, a Christmas card was received at the Bronner's home in the early 1980s.

The card was designed by Virginia Witt, wife of Rev. Elmer Witt, executive director of the organization. With the help of Dr. Oswald Hoffmann the message on the card was edited and shortened into a mission statement reading:

"Enjoy CHRISTmas, It's HIS Birthday

Enjoy LIFE, It's HIS Way."

The motto is appreciated by many as it appears on our building, billboards, stationery and many advertisements.

12 | Tributes to Staff, Suppliers, Guests and Media

The Bronner family is very thankful for the thousands of dedicated staff members who have worked at Bronner's through the years. They have been an integral part of Bronner's growth into the world's largest Christmas store.

The Bronner group works hard and enjoys social celebrations as well. In the early years, there were two parties per year. One party even included an all-staff musical ensemble with Irene at the piano and Wally playing his saxophone. A special tradition for the staff each year is the annual Christmas party, held "early" . . . during January . . . an ideal time to party in a relaxed manner following the rush of a busy season. Each year since 1964, the theme of the Christmas party has centered on a particular nation. A sampling of themes includes CHRISTmas in the Styles of the British Isles, CHRISTmas with a Touch of Dutch, a Hungarian CHRISTmas Rhapsody, a Brazil CHRISTmas Thrill, Canadian CHRISTmas Capers, a CHRISTmas Wonder Down Under, and a Polynesian CHRISTmas. In the 1976 bicentennial year, the theme was our own United States. For the 50th year of the business, the Christmas party theme was a Salute to the Bronner Stars and the STAR of Stars. Christmas in Bethlehem was the timely theme for the year 2000. Each year staff members receive literature about the Christmas customs and traditions of the select nation, and some guests even arrive at the party in appropriate ethnic attire. In keeping with the theme, the décor accents customs and characteristics of the featured nation. Attendance has grown to 600.

The Bronner family annually invites staff members' young children and their parents to a Christmas party. Santa gives a gift to each child. Since 1977 the children's parties have been held in the program center.

The Bronners are most thankful for the many loyal staff members (over 3,500) who have shared their talents with the

Bronner organization throughout its history. Wally shares the following statements with Bronner staff members during training sessions for newcomers and general meetings of the Bronner team:

Our organization consists of leaders rather than bosses. Every team member is a leader who leads themselves with the mind and others with the heart.

The Bronner family does, however, acknowledge that they have a boss . . . the good Lord. Their goal is for the business to be led in a Lord-pleasing way throughout each day.

"Let's strive for #1!"

"Every person that enters BRONNER'S CHRISTmas WONDERLAND is considered to be a #1 guest . . . that has made a special effort to visit a #1 establishment . . . staffed with a #1 team that offers #1 service and a #1 variety of decorations and gifts displayed in a #1 manner . . . all of this hopefully pleasing to the ultimate #1 . . . the good Lord."

The entire Bronner team realizes that each visit and purchase by a guest is a vote for the business to continue.

The Bronners also appreciate the many suppliers who have provided quality merchandise for the world's largest Christmas store over the years. They look forward to continuing the many, fine working relationships that have developed and to establishing new connections.

Members of the media have provided generous coverage of BRONNER'S CHRISTmas WONDERLAND in local, regional, national, and international newspapers, trade publications, journals, resource books, magazines, and radio and television programing. Radio coverage has included newscasts, documentaries, Christmas programs, talk shows, and call-in programs from as far away as Europe and Africa. Television reports have included Bronner's for travel, Christmas décor, and Christmas customs accents; Silent Night Chapel features; settings for religious programs; and ambiance for performing artists.

Tributes to Staff

Nautical, summertime relaxation in the 1950s.

WE APPRECIATE OUR GREAT STAFF AND GUESTS!

THE BRONNER FAMILY

Staff member and sailor, **DALE "MUNCHY" MUEHLFELD**, stops in to say "hi" in the early 1970s. (l-r) Front row: Pat Neeley, Munchy, Jan Kribs. Back row: Irene Veitengruber, June Auernhammer, Joanne Goldammer, June Finger, Fritzie Hill, and Kay Finkbeiner.

The Bronner family presents a retirement gift to **VERNA DUBKE** - always a sad and glad occasion.

Irene and Wally recognize **EDDIE BEYERLEIN,** the first team member to work 25 years for Bronner's, pictured with his mother, Ida Beyerlein, and wife Jane.

A treat for the Bronner staff moms!

Themed Christmas Parties

1983, in Hawaiian attire (l-r) Wayne and Lorene Bronner, Maria Bronner (front), Carla Bronner, Wally and Irene Bronner, Randy Bronner.

1975 - USA Bicentennial - Wally and Irene portray George and Martha Washington. Annual staff parties in ethnic themes acquaint the team with varied cuisine and customs.

1979 (India)

1992 (Spanish theme and 500th Anniversary of America's discovery)

1995 was a special year. 150th Anniversary of Frankenmuth and 50th Anniversary of Bronner's store. Wally and Irene with family (l-r) Chris and Maria Bronner Sutorik, Wayne and Lorene Bronner, Bob and Carla Bronner Spletzer.

...More Christmas Parties

1999 Bethlehem

2002 Alpine Christmas

2002 staff anniversarians. (clockwise from top) Fred Beyerlein, Anne Koehler, Elaine Peters, Mary Ellen Schoenow, Joanne Brewer, Kevin Maurer, Connie Larsen.

2003 Caribbean Christmas anniversarians with Wally and Irene Bronner. Standing (l to r): Jeanne Braeutigam, Donna Rupprecht. Seated: Wally, Karen Hoffman, Dennis Pfund, Sharon Bierlein, Irene.

Bronner's Program Center

Guests enjoy Christmas sing-a-long on December 22nd and 23rd. **IRENE** at the old-fashioned, parlor pump organ. **WALLY** and **BOB SPLETZER** direct the singing.

PAUL, GREG AND RYAN SPLETZER hold the ornament of the year, a gift at the party. In preparation for the party, children color pictures of the annual ornament.

Children of staff members are hosted at an early December **CHRISTMAS PARTY**.

TRIBUTES TO STAFF, SUPPLIERS, GUESTS AND MEDIA

Wishes Fulfilled

MRS. BEULAH SIMS ON A SHOPPING SPREE with all of her 10 daughters on her 85th birthday. Standing: Connie Dunne, Shirley Davis, Carolyn Weigel, Marilyn Davis, Sharon Armstrong, Janet Watts. Kneeling: Nancy Sims, Donna Hyland, Beulah Sims, Darlene Jewell and Jeannie Collins.

SIX CHRISTMAS-SHOPPING SISTERS dressed alike visit Bronner's. Harriette Knaup, Betty Gross, Rosemary Campbell, Virginia Williams, Dolly Peterson, Joan Reuther.

LITTLE LINDSEY CROSS VISITED BRONNER'S AFTER HER BONE MARROW TRANSPLANT. Front: Chantelle & Tiana Cross. Back: Mike Hollenbeck ("Saginaw News" photographer), friends holding Brittany, Dean Bohn ("Saginaw News" reporter), Jeremy Cross holding Lindsey, Christiana Cross & Roselle McCormic.

Thanks to the Media

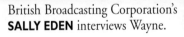

WUGN Christian Radio often broadcasts from Bronner's.

WSGW radio personalities **ART LEWIS** and **SUSAN SMITH** host Christmas shows in Bronner's Season's Eatings area.

WNEM TV5's **LENISE LIGON** interviews Wally.

British Broadcasting Corporation's **SALLY EDEN** interviews Wayne.

Radio host **PAUL W. SMITH** and weatherman **JOHN MCMURRAY** chat with Wally about Christmas customs.

...And More Thanks

NBC's **MIKE LEONARD** (with **WAYNE BRONNER** and **CARLA BRONNER SPLETZER**) prepared a feature that aired on the Today Show on December 25, 1997.

JOHN CZARNECKI and **LEANNE GOVITZ** of Davenport University chat with honored alumnus **DR. WALLY BRONNER** on WEYI TV25.

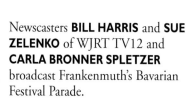

Fox Network remote broadcasts from Bronner's Silent Night Chapel.

Newscasters **BILL HARRIS** and **SUE ZELENKO** of WJRT TV12 and **CARLA BRONNER SPLETZER** broadcast Frankenmuth's Bavarian Festival Parade.

EARLY STORIES ABOUT BRONNER'S - Articles about our Christmas business appeared in many newspapers and the following magazines:

"Standard Torch" - 1956   "Today's Business" - 1966
"Coronet" - 1957   "Toys & Novelty" - 1968
"This Day" - 1958   "Retail & Business Review" - 1970
"Michigan Bell" - 1965   "Ford Times" - 1972
"AAA Motor News" - 1965

ANNUAL FORM ORNAMENT - In 2000, Bronner's designed and produced their first annual form ornament.

PROFIT SHARING - In 1981, the Bronner family developed a profit-sharing program to encourage exceptional staff performance and increase profits. While the Bronner family and staff realize profits are never guaranteed, the profit-sharing program and other contributing factors have resulted in annual profits that are shared with staff who qualify.

BEAMER THE BRONNER STAR - Bronner's promotions team developed Beamer the Bronner Star™ in 1999 to serve as Bronner's mascot.

WALLY THE LEADER DOG - Cynthia Klein from Utica, Michigan, is a trainer for the Lions Club seeing eye dog program. She surprised Wally in 2003 by naming one of her dogs "Wally" in recognition of Wally being a charter member of the Frankenmuth Lions Club.

13 | Honors for Bronner's

During Bronner's first sixty years of entrepreneurship, the business has received many recognitions, presentations, and awards. Trophies and plaques are not a goal. Each tribute, however, makes us mindful that the combination of guests and quality staff performance is the lifeline to a successful business. Although Bronner's features approximately 6,000 styles of ornaments, the most appreciated ornaments are first-time and repeat guests and the ever-increasing number of loyal families and groups that make visits to Frankenmuth and Bronner's CHRISTmas Wonderland a tradition, and those who visit Bronner's website and shop from Bronner's catalog.

A cross-section of awards include the following:

- 2005 Named as Michigan Retailer of the Year
- 2005 U.S. Postal Service Potter Award for most improved company by postal standards (presentation by U.S. Postmaster Jack Potter)
- 2004 NMA (National Management Association) Hall of Fame Award sponsored by Blue Cross Blue Shield
- 2003 Selected Retailer Award GCA (Garden Centers of America) Holiday Garden Center Tour
  - 2003 Travel Michigan Outstanding Achievement in Michigan Tourism Award
- 2003 Saginaw County Convention & Visitors Bureau Pinnacle Award
- 2002 Wallace J. Bronner Excellence in Business Award from Davenport University
- 2002 Christus Vivit Award from Concordia Seminary - St. Louis, Missouri
- 2001 Inspirational Giftware National Impact in Ministry Award
- 2001 Silver Good Citizenship Medal & Flag Certificate from the Paul Emory Chapter of the Sons of the American Revolution
- 2001 N.O.E.L. (National Ornaments and Electric Lights Christmas Association) 2001 Retailer of the Year - Specialty Store Year-Round, 1994 Hall of Fame, 1981 Retailer of the Year

- 2000 Tribute from Frankenmuth American Legion for Honoring Veterans
- 2000 MDA Spirit of Sharing Award presented to Wally & Irene
- 2000 American Tract Society Award presented to Wally & Irene
- 1999 Junior Achievement Fellows Award
- 1999 Silver Medal of Honor for Arts, Culture, and Religion (from the governor of the state of Salzburg, Austria)
- 1998 Davenport College Honorary Doctor of Letters Degree (for commitment to education, contributions to the community, and support of Davenport University – formerly Saginaw Business Institute – and its mission)
- 1998 Goebel National Retailer of the Year Award
- 1997 Blue Chip Enterprise Initiative National Award (from U.S. Chamber of Commerce, MassMutual, Nation's Business, and "First Business")
- 1997 Goebel Retailer of the Year Award for the Midwest Region
- 1997 Saginaw Rescue Mission Friend of the Friendless Award
- 1997 All Area Arts Award (for significant contributions through the arts to the quality of life in Saginaw County)
- 1996 Frank N. Andersen Spirit of Philanthropy Award
- 1995 Michigan Master Entrepreneur of the Year Award
- 1993 Lions Club International Foundation Melvin Jones Fellow
- 1993 AAA-Chicago "Travel Treasure"
- 1992 Saginaw County Community Improvement Award
- 1992, 1991, & 1990 Keep Michigan Beautiful Award
- 1989 Rotary International Paul Harris Fellowship Award
- 1988 Salvation Army Others Award
- 1988 Frankenmuth Jaycees Herbert L. Keinath Community Service Award
- 1986 Concordia Lutheran Seminary - Fort Wayne, Indiana Christian Service Award presented to Wally & Irene Bronner
- 1986 Golden Santa Claus Award (Nuremberg International Fair)
- 1985 AAA-Michigan "One of Top-Ten Man-made Attractions in Michigan"
- 1976 Embassy for Michigan Tourism (by governor)

Recognitions

Muscular Dystrophy Association, Salvation Army, Davenport University, Toys for Tots, and the NOEL Association are among groups that have accorded tributes to Bronner's.

Salvation Army **COLONELS CLARENCE** and **LOIS HARVEY** present Others Award to Wally and Irene in 1988.

Numerous awards are in Bronner's salesroom exhibit cases.

President **RON SCHOENFELD**, presents NOEL Award to **CARLA**; and **WALLY** in 1981.

In 1998 Davenport University accorded an **HONORARY DOCTOR OF LETTERS DEGREE TO WALLY**. Concordia Seminary/St. Louis presented him with a **CHRISTUS VIVIT AWARD** in 2002. Concordia Seminary/Ft. Wayne recognized **IRENE WITH THE PRISCILLA AWARD** and **WALLY WITH THE MILLES CHRISTI AWARD**.

DR. BARBARA MIERAS, IRENE, WALLY &
PRESIDENT RANDOLPH FLECHSIG - 2002

CHRISTMAS DECORATIONS MAGAZINES - Publications including "Selling Christmas Decorations," "Festival Christmas," "Celebrate 365," and "Creche Herald" have showcased Bronner's.

WALLY IN WASHINGTON, D.C. - Wally was elected in 1979 as a Michigan delegate to President Carter's White House Conference on Small Business. In 1995 he served as a delegate to the first White House Conference on Tourism when President Clinton was in office.

YES! IT'S TRUE - At Bronner's visitors can see a currency display featuring one low denomination note from every country in the world. The latest addition was East Timor.

Also to be seen are stamps on corners of envelopes from round the world correspondence.

A poster board is on display showing photos of license plates from every state and province from USA and Canada and some from Mexico. By far, most photos were snapped in Bronner's parking lot.

KEEP MICHIGAN BEAUTIFUL - In 1991, Phyllis Brooks of Dearborn, Michigan, nominated Bronner's CHRISTmas Wonderland for a Keep Michigan Beautiful Award. Bronner's received additional KMB awards in 1994 and 2002.

14 | Caring and Sharing

The giving motivation of the Bronner family is based on Biblical teachings found in II Corinthians 9: 6-7 and Matthew 25.

"Remember this: The person who plants (sows) sparingly will harvest (reap) sparingly; and the person who plants with expressions of praise and thanks will harvest with expressions of praise and thanks. Let each person do what he has decided in his heart, not grudgingly or as a result of pressure, because God loves a cheerful giver." (II Corinthians 9: 6-7)

"For I was hungry, and you gave Me something to eat; I was thirsty, and you gave Me a drink; I was a stranger, and you took Me into your homes; naked, and you gave Me something to wear; sick, and you looked after Me; in prison, and you visited Me . . . And the King will answer them, 'I tell you the truth, anything you did for one of My brothers here, even the least important of them, you did for Me.'" (Matthew 25: 35, 36, & 40)

"God has blessed the Bronner family beyond our fondest expectations," said Irene. "He sent His only-begotten Son to be mankind's Savior from sin and to assure us of a place with him in heaven forevermore. Out of gratitude for His great love for us, we wanted to share."

Each year the Wallace and Irene Bronner Family Charitable Foundation, established on December 28, 1966, receives more than 1,000 requests for donations.

"Annually we contribute to over 400 causes, including 125 within Saginaw County," said Wally. "In addition we fund the total annual costs for maintenance of the Silent Night Memorial Chapel, which was built and paid for in 1992. Our gifting is primarily for Christian outreach, predominantly within the Lutheran church and its many programs. We also give to educational, medical, social, and humanitarian efforts for the truly needy, as well as to veteran, civic, cultural, and historical causes in our extended communities."

The Bronner family made a major contribution to the construction of the Frankenmuth Public School's Performing Arts Center that was dedicated in 2002.

The family also contributed to the all-new dining hall in the St. Lorenz Lutheran school addition dedicated in fall of 2004.

Giving and sharing are a three-fold blessing:

One, the joy of having something to give . . . time, talents, or monetary gifts.

Two, the joy of sharing so others can be helped.

Three, the joy of realizing the benefits others are receiving from the gifts.

There are additional blessings because others may be inspired to contribute in the manner of their choice with their resources.

Bronner's team members regularly give at blood drives and food drives and to organizations such as the Muscular Dystrophy Association, World Vision, American Red Cross, Salvation Army, Lutheran World Relief, Catholic World Relief, Coats for Kids, and Toys for Tots. During November and December and during catastrophes, Bronner's matches (up to $100 per staff member) gifts for recognized charitable organizations serving humanitarian needs.

Visitations, meditations, and celebrations... there were many times to smile, laugh, praise, cry, and pray as the Bronner family worked with over 3,500 individual team members throughout the years. While in attendance at weddings, anniversaries, births/birthdays, graduations, retirements, hospital stays, and funerals, this popular phrase served as the family's guide: No one cares how much you know, but knowing how much you care is important.

The Bronner family was blessed with the chance to become better acquainted with staff members and their extended families on these occasions. Visits to hospital rooms and funeral homes offered meaningful moments to share with each other the comforts of the Christian faith.

The Bronners first experienced the death of a staff member in the 1950s, the early days of the sign business, when a youthful Bruce Bartlett died from illness. At the 121 East Tuscola Street location, the family and staff were saddened by the early death of Kay Finkbeiner in 1975. At the all-new location, Bronner's first staff member to enter heaven was Sandy Corwin, as the result of cancer, in the 1980s.

"We thank God for all that those dear people meant to their families and co-workers, and that they knew their Savior," Wally said.

"It is not unusual to be asked about problems I have encountered throughout the history of the business," Wally said. "Regular prayer at the beginning of family, board, managerial, and supervisory meetings always set the proper frame of mind for handling challenges in a Lord-pleasing manner."

Anne Koehler, long-time Bronner's manager, has said, "We must fill our minds with so many positive thoughts that any negative thoughts will starve."

Were there times of stress?

"Yes!" said Wally. "But stress is healthy when it is dealt with properly and not allowed to turn into distress." Another thought about stressed...when reversed...turns into desserts.

Bronner's faced a major challenge in 1976 and 1977 when the relocation process was underway. However, everyone worked together to deal with construction, sign production, shutting down the three old stores, and moving to and opening the massive store at the new site.

"Always of comfort were the three verses of the hymn, 'What a Friend We Have in Jesus,' which bear the repetitive phrase, 'take it to the Lord in prayer,'" Wally said.

Community Activity

The **BETHLEHEM SCENE** on riverbank serves as a community Christmas card to all.

The **FRANKENMUTH BEAUTIFICATION COMMITTEE** (Wally is a 1955 charter member) posed with the "2000" display.

CARING AND SHARING

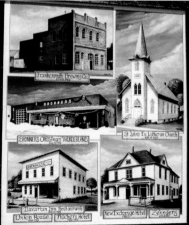

BRONNER'S CONTRIBUTES TO COMMUNITY PROJECTS including Christmas decorations and Frankenmuth Historical Museum's building addition and exhibits.

Caring & Sharing

The Bronner family made major contributions toward **FRANKENMUTH HIGH SCHOOL PERFORMING ARTS CENTER** and **ST. LORENZ SCHOOL DINING HALL.**

Bronner's helped **CHILDREN IN BETHLEHEM** receive presents for Christmas 2000.

The Bronner family contributed toward the replication of **FRANKENMUTH'S FIRST MILL.**

Bronner's funded challenge grants for first permanent home of **MICHIGAN'S OWN MILITARY AND SPACE MUSEUM.**

WILL YOU MARRY ME? - Bronner's is pleased that our store and chapel can serve a special place for the lover's question to be popped... "will you marry me?"

Some speak the words in a remote corner of the salesroom, others in the Silent Night Chapel or on the outside steps. Still others choose not to speak but merely have the words of proposal hand lettered on an ornament and discreetly placed on a Christmas tree...waiting for screams of joy from the hopeful bride-to-be.

MEMORABILIA SHARED Often special people remember us by bringing to our attention an early item we may have produced and forgotten, but would appreciate rediscovering.

In particular we are thankful for Doc McCray and Mary McCray Sovey who made it possible for us to add to our program center collection one of the very first 24" x 48" hardboard, Christmas-themed panels that we produced for the J.P. Ippel Company of Saginaw.

Thoughtful Robert Rundell helped us obtain the first cut-out, life-sized Nativity scene that Wally painted for the lawn of St. Lorenz Lutheran School on Main Street - ordered at that time for the Gera Dramatic Walther League Youth Group.

The family of barber Ed Daenzer returned to Wally what probably was the first showcard sign that he painted and the list goes on...

15 Community Involvement

Wally thanks God for good health and encouragement from his dear wife Irene and family that has allowed him to participate in a wide range of community affairs. (He believes community can be local, regional, national, and international.) Although some inform Wally that they have benefited from his involvement, he is of the opinion that he has gained far more from others than he has been able to give in return.

Statements that have greatly influenced Wally over the years include the following:

- "Search for a joyful vocation where you might tire of long hours but never of the job." – Dr. Clem Kirchgeorg
- "Do something about it." – Wally's wife Irene
- "Share your God-given talents." – Dr. Oswald Hoffman
- "Christians meet in the gathered church for an hour weekly and in the scattered church daily." – Rev. Elmer Witt
- "Wherever there is a Christian, there is a missionary, and wherever there is a missionary, there is a mission field." – Dr. William Kohn
- "Volunteerism is what makes America great, and the lack of it can ruin America." – Governor George Romney
- "Christians must live their faith." – President Jimmy Carter
- "YOU, the veterans, are the HEROES of yesterday, the HEROES of today, and the HEROES of tomorrow." – General John Shalikashvili
- "The main thing about faith is that the main thing is always the main thing." – Rev. Dale Ahlschwede
- "Christians must WALK THE TALK of Christian faith." – President George W. Bush
- Media personalities Bill Edwards, Howard Wolf and Bob Chandler advised business managers to meet and greet many people.

Wally's National and International Community Involvement
- International president of the Walther League (young people's organization of the Lutheran church)
- Christmas decorations enthusiast and speaker
- Volunteerism promoter and speaker
- Tourism delegate to the first-ever White House Tourism Conference
- Speaker for various Christian causes

Wally's Regional Community Involvement
- Honorary Chairman for American Cancer Society Holiday Card campaign; American Lung Association Christmas Seals; and Toys for Tots
- Salvation Army Kettle Campaign chairs for Michigan and Northern Indiana (Wally and Irene)
- State of Michigan Lutheran Children's Friend Society Centennial Campaign co-chairs (Wally and Irene)
- Greater Saginaw Foundation's campaign co-chair to match a million dollar challenge grant from the Kresge Foundation
- Member of Gideon International - Pat Zondervan, former International President, sponsored Wally

Wally's Local Community Involvement
- Numerous church committees, offices, and campaigns
- Graphics committees for the 100th, 125th, and 150th Anniversaries of Frankenmuth
- Charter member of the City of Frankenmuth Beautification Committee (1955)
- Charter member of Frankenmuth Lions Club

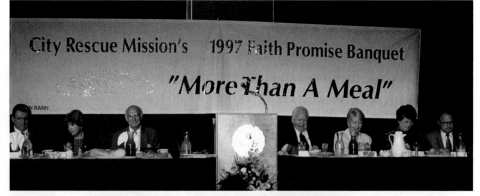

Bronner's Participates in Many Charitable Activities

Wally was a speaker at the inaugural convention for **FRIENDS OF THE CRECHE**. He gives up to 250 speeches per year.

Springhill Suites manager **KAREN DICE ACCEPTS BIBLES FROM GIDEONS**. Seated: Don Weber. Standing: John Abraham, Kim Cederberg, Ed Beyerlein, Earl Palmreuter, Bill Varney, George Roenicke, Irving Reinbold, Richard Krafft, Jr. & Wally Bronner.

Sponsor of Choral Society Concert

Red Cross Awards Event

Wally & Irene... Grand Marshals

Lansing, Michigan's **MAYOR & MRS. HOLLISTER** greet parade marshals Irene and Wally at Parade of Lights.

CANADIAN THANKSGIVING AND OKTOBERFEST PARADE in Kitchener - Waterloo, Ontario

LT. GOV. DICK POSTHUMUS and parade marshals **IRENE** and **WALLY** at the Frankenmuth Bavarian Festival

Wally with sister-in-law **JUNE BRONNER** at Saginaw Lions Park. Bronner's made a contribution in honor of brother Arnold, Lion and Army veteran.

Honorary Chair and Promoter of Toys for Tots

Frankenmuth Lions Highway Cleanup team **WALLY, BILL MOSSNER, LARRY FOWLER, BILL VARNEY, MARK PANKNER** and **MARVIN SPERLING**

16 Well-Known People We Met

Over the years we met many celebrities at Bronner's and/or elsewhere. In fact, Wally feels privileged to have met every President from Dwight Eisenhower through George W. Bush (except Lyndon B. Johnson) and every Michigan governor from G. Mennen Williams through Jennifer Granholm.

Before 1976
Dr. Oswald Hoffman, "Lutheran Hour" host
Marvin Herzog, Polka Hall of Fame
Dick Gregory - comedian, actor, author, recording artist, and civil rights activist
Ann Landers, syndicated columnist

1976
John Wayne (ordered Santa suit by phone), actor
Maria von Trapp, von Trapp Family Singers
Nelson Rockefeller, governor of New York, vice president of the United States of America

1979
Norma and Randy Zimmer, Guy & Ralna, Bobby Burgess, Sandi Griffiths, and Mary Lou Metzger - "Lawrence Welk Show"
Albert Thewalt, German stein producer

1980
Juan Fernandiz, Spanish artist

1982
Conway Twitty, country western singer/musician
Dr. James Kennedy, Coral Ridge Ministries
David Brinkley, national television news anchor
Pat Robertson, televangelist

1983

Mr. & Mrs. Joseph Field, Marshall Field's department store
Florence & Debbie Hansen, Hansen Singing Strings
Debra Sue Maffett, Miss America 1983
Milt Wilcox, Detroit Tigers pitcher
The Lennon Sisters, "Lawrence Welk Show"
Van Johnson, actor
William Conrad, actor
Buddy Ebsen, actor

1984

Annie Fitzgerald, Irish artist
Tom and Marge Monaghan, Domino's Pizza originator and owner of
    Detroit Tigers baseball team
Andy Williams, singer
Ted Nugent, singer/musician
Terry Bailey, Miss Dominion of Canada 1984
Tom Netherton, gospel singer
Jerry Mathers, the Beaver of "Leave It to Beaver"
Princess Grace and Prince Rainier III of Monaco
Kevin Leman, Christian counselor and author
Randy Carlson, Christian counselor and author
Warren and Char Bolthouse, founders of Family Life Radio
Morry and Dorothy Carlson, founders of Youth Haven Ranch

1985

Michigan Governor James Blanchard
Ruth and Robert Miller, Hummel authorities
Bo and Millie Schembechler and son Schemmie, U of M football coach
Dr. & Mrs. Ken Taylor, "Living Bible" translator
Hugo Fontanini, Fontanini creche producer
Clara Scroggins, Christmas ornament authority
Sam Butcher and Bill Biel, Precious Moments artists
Myron Floren, Lawrence Welk Orchestra accordionist
Gordon McRae, singer
Irene Vermeulen, Miss Dominion of Canada 1985
Anne Burt, wife of the late musician and composer Alfred Burt
Lance Parish, Detroit Tigers catcher
Warren Pierce, Detroit radio broadcaster

1986

Carmel Quinn, singer and storyteller
Dennis Day, actor

1986 (continued)
Jerry Murad & the Harmonicats, mouth organ trio
Marie Osmond and son - singer, actress, doll designer, and co-founder/co-host of Children's Miracle Network

1987
Lowell Davis, artist
The Lettermen: Tony Butila, Mark Preston, Donovan Scott Tea - singers
Dale Evans – actress, singer, and author
Gigi Graham Tchividjion, Dr. Billy & Ruth Graham's daughter
Anita Bryant – Miss Oklahoma, singer, actress, spokesperson, and political activist
Allison Lewis, 1987 Miss Dominion of Canada
Frank Yankovic, America's Polka King
Joe Finney, "Lawrence Welk Show"
Paul Harvey, national radio broadcaster
Michigan Lt. Governor Jim Brickley

1988
Gerhard Skrobek, Hummel figurine master sculptor
Grennady Stekalov, Russian cosmonaut
Linda Farrell, 1988 Miss Dominion of Canada
Gene Riley, Christian singer
Gene Shallot, film critic
Erma Bombeck, comedian and author

1989
Lt. Colonel Clarence and Lois Harvey, Salvation Army
Ben Kinchelow, Christian Broadcasting Network
Dan Rather, national television news anchor for CBS
Arthur Frommer, travel editor
Max Duncan, artist
Christian Steinbach, leading nutcracker producer
Ernie Harwell, Detroit Tigers baseball announcer
Emmett Kelly, Jr. – world-renowned clown

1990
Ink Spots, singers/musicians
Pat Paulsen, comedian
Willie Horton, Detroit Tigers

1991

Pat Boone, singer

Michael Moore, movie producer

Chuck Colson, Prison Fellowship Ministries

Art Buchwald – humorist, syndicated columnist, author, Pulitzer Prize winner

1992

Paula Zahn of CBS

Roy Clark, country music singer/musician

Steve and Jayne Meadows Allen – TV personality, author, composer

Victor Borge – humorist, entertainer, world-class pianist

Arthur Duncan, tap dancer

Senator Paul Simon

Sandi Patti, Christian singer

President and Mrs. Jimmy Carter

General Norman Schwarzkopf

David Dravecky, baseball role model

Little Jimmy Dickens, country/western musician

Mayor Raimund Traintinger and Mayor Andres Kinzl of Oberndorf, Austria

Michigan Governor John and Michelle Engler

1993

Dorothy Hamill, Olympic skater

Gene Freedman, Enesco Corporation founder

Christian and Guenther Ulbricht, nutcracker producers

Michigan Governor George W. and Mrs. Romney

Louise Mandrell, country/western musician

Charlton Heston, actor

Oprah Winfrey, entertainment executive

Margaret Thatcher, British Prime Minister

Shari Lewis, ventriloquist, children's educational television, musician, conductor

Dr. Maya Angelou, poet/author

Jim Nabors, actor and singer

Eva Burrows, Salvation Army world general

Cal Thomas – political analyst, syndicated columnist, and radio show host

Deacon Bernie, impersonator of St. Nicholas

1994

Smothers Brothers (Tom and Dick) – comedians

David Coulier, actor

Doc Severinsen, bandleader for over 25 years on the "Tonight Show" with Johnny Carson

Michigan Lt. Governor Connie Binsfeld

James Earl Jones, actor

Jack and Gratia Lousma, United States astronaut

Vice President Dan Quayle

Archbishop Desmond Tutu

Jeanne Cooper of "Young and the Restless"

Dr. Robert Schuller, Crystal Cathedral Ministries and author

1995

Robert and Sharon Brenner, authors

Jeanne-Marie Dickens, great-great-granddaughter by marriage of Charles Dickens

J. P. McCarthy, WJR radio host

Thomas and Marlene Horn, glass ornament artisans

Joni Eareckson Tada, author and founder of "Joni and Friends" radio program

1996

Michigan's First Lady Michelle Engler and triplet daughters Madeleine, Margaret and Hannah

Interviewed by Harry Smith, Jane Robelot, and Mark McEwen of "CBS This Morning"

President Bill Clinton, Vice President Al Gore

Ann Jillian – actress, singer, and motivational speaker

Lisa Robertson, Paul Kelly, Dan Hughes, QVC Channel

Eddie Walker, woodcarver

Patrick Simmons, Disney sculptor

Michigan Secretary of State Candace Miller

Bob Dole, 1996 presidential candidate, vice-presidential candidate Jack Kemp

1997

Mike Leonard, NBC "Today Show"

Al Unser, Jr., auto racer

Ambassador Allan Keyes

Rick Barrett, Fox TV

Emanuele Fontanini, Fontanini crèche producer

1997 (continued)
Faith Hill, country/western singer
Paul Smith, Detroit radio personality
Sergei Fedorov, Detroit Red Wings center
Maria von Trapp (daughter of Maria von Trapp), von Trapp Family
    Singers
Phyllis Wallace, "Woman to Woman" radio program host
Vienna Boys Choir
Dr. Dale Meyer, "Main Street" TV host
Diamond Dallas Page, wrestler
Bill Anderson, author
Carol Duvall, TV crafter

1998
Mr. & Mrs. Hockey, Gordie and Colleen Howe
Dell Vaughn, "Michigan Magazine"
Bob Heft, designer of USA flag
Burt Bacharach, musician
Polly Bergen, actress
Bob Colletta, Buick president
Don Warning, Santa historian
Lt. Colonel Michael Bloomfield, United States astronaut
Dr. Lloyd Ogilvie, U.S. Senate chaplain
Dr. Paul Maier, historian and theologian
Jerry Linenger, United States astronaut
Thomas "Hitman" Hearns, boxer
Marla Maples Trump, actress

1999
Garth and Tina Coonce, Tri State Christian TV
Bob and Joyce Byers, creators of Byers' Choice Carolers
Ana Cani, "Lawrence Welk Show" vocalist
Chris Sheedy, Simon Banks, Teymoor Nabili of British Broadcasting
Maria Garcia and Jimmy Barrios of "Serenatas Latinas"
Sally Eden of "Good Morning Britain"
Twila Paris, Christian vocalist, and sister Starla
Rosmarie von Trapp, von Trapp Family Singers
Richard Simmons, fitness expert
Julia Child, chef and author
General Colin Powell
Frederick Baker, British Broadcasting Corporation
First Lady Laura Bush

2000

Gaylord Ho, Seraphim master sculptor
Christian Goebel, Goebel factory
Mahima Chaudary and Manoj Bajpi, Indian film stars
Elisabeth von Trapp, singer
Dr. Robert Schuller, Jr. - Crystal Cathedral Ministries
von Trapp children, singers
Parker Bohn III, PBA champ

2001

Glenn Haege, America's master handyman
Cindy Williams, "Laverne and Shirley"
The Hubcaps, '50s band
Marco Fontanini, Fontanini crèche producer
Thurlow Spurr, musician/conductor/producer/director
Stephen Strang, Strang Publications
Bob Jones, Jr., Bob Jones University
Charles Osgood, national news anchor and author
Dr. James Dobson, founder of Focus on the Family Ministries

2002

Sam Donaldson, national broadcast journalist
Vice President Al & Tipper Gore
Art Linkletter, broadcast host
Michigan Lt. Governor Dick Posthumus
Jim Govan, Friends of the Creche president
Rita Bocher, "Creche Herald" editor
Dr. Barbara Mieras, Davenport University Foundation president
Randolph Flechsig, Davenport University president
Alessandro Fontanini, Fontanini crèche producers
Jimmy Sturr, Grammy-winning polka musician
Susan Cherry, ornament designer

2003

Al Roker, national NBC weatherman and author
Rev. Kenneth Klaus, "International Lutheran Hour" speaker
Alan Harre, Valparaiso University president
Michigan Governor Jennifer Granholm
James Carville, political strategist and consultant
Mary Matalin, political strategist and consultant

2003 *(continued)*
Ernie Harwell, baseball broadcaster
Michigan Attorney General Michael Cox
Michigan Secretary of State Terri Lynn Land
Brent Bodine, NASCAR racer
Kausha Rach and Sandeep Batchu, Indian film stars
Michigan Lt. Governor John Cherry
Jack Greene, Grand Ole Opry singer
Candi Carpenter, country singer

2004
Horst Hoefler, Hummel master painter
Carleton Fisk, baseball hall of famer
Lem Barney, pro football hall of famer
Tara Reid, actress
Terry Bradshaw, pro football hall of famer
Dr. Tim Johnson, medical advisor
Jack Canfield and Mark Victor Hansen, authors of Chicken Soup books

2005
Rudy Giuliani, 107th mayor of New York City
Pastor Jack Hayford, theologian & author
Mike Wallace, TV Journalist
Dan Peek, author, songwriter, musician
Max Lucado, author
Michael W. Smith, singer
Jeff Obafemi Carr, actor
Gary & Barbara Chapman, author
Dennis Rainey, author
Bobby Vinton, singer
Lou Holtz, college football coach & motivational speaker
Ulrich Tendera, Goebel master artist

Well-Known People

Our years in business have provided opportunities to meet many notables at conferences, tradeshows, concerts, airports and in our store.

President George H. Bush

President Bill Clinton

President Ronald Reagan

Paul Simon
U.S. Senator

Spencer Abraham
U.S. Secretary of Energy

Vice President Al Gore

Irene and Wally greet **Laura Bush**,
wife of President George W. Bush, at Bronner's.

President George W. Bush

WELL-KNOWN PEOPLE

193

Jerry Linenger, Astronaut/Cosmonaut

General Norman Schwarzkopf

Charles Osgood
CBS Newsman

Carla Bronner Spletzer with
newscaster **Paul Harvey**

James Brickley
Michigan Lieutenant Governor

**Elizabeth
Dole**
U.S. Senator

Glenn Haege
America's Master
Handyman

Photos of numerous dignitaries adorn **Bronner's walls**

Hands of Welcome are Extended to Guests and Groups

RED HAT SOCIETIES visit Christmas Wonderland.

The **CHARLES W. HOWARD SANTA SCHOOL** in Midland, Michigan, visits Bronner's annually.

195

Jennifer Granholm
Michigan Governor

Jim Blanchard
Michigan Governor

William Milliken
Michigan Governor

George Romney
Michigan Governor

Lt. Gov. Connie Binsfeld and
husband **John**

Michigan Governor **John Engler's wife Michelle Engler** and
their triplet daughters **Madeleine, Margaret and Hannah**

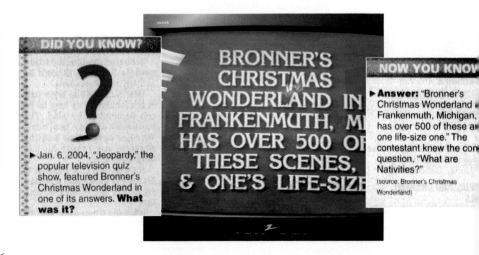

DID YOU KNOW?

?

▶ Jan. 6, 2004, "Jeopardy," the
popular television quiz
show, featured Bronner's
Christmas Wonderland in
one of its answers. **What
was it?**

BRONNER'S
CHRISTMAS
WONDERLAND IN
FRANKENMUTH, MI
HAS OVER 500 OF
THESE SCENES,
& ONE'S LIFE-SIZE

NOW YOU KNOW

▶ **Answer:** "Bronner's
Christmas Wonderland
Frankenmuth, Michigan,
has over 500 of these a
one life-size one." The
contestant knew the cor
question, "What are
Nativities?"
(source: Bronner's Christmas
Wonderland)

196

Irene meets **Gigi Tchividjan**, Billy Graham's daughter.

Joni Eareckson Tada
Artist and Christian Commentator

Ken Taylor
Translator of the
"Living Bible"

Harry Smith
Newscaster

Marlin Maddox
Newscaster

Dr. James Dobson
Christian counselor

T.D. Jakes
Evangelist/bishop

Ted Johnson
Talk show host

Mike Redford
Newscaster

Dr. Dale Meyer
Theologian

Dr. James E. Kennedy
Evangelist/pastor

Dr. Robert Schuller
"Hour of Power" founder

Dr. Oswald Hoffman
"Lutheran Hour" speaker

WELL-KNOWN PEOPLE

197

TV Crafter Extraordinaire **Carol Duvall**

Art Linkletter TV Personality

Mark McEwen
Newscaster

TV personality **Williard Scott** visited Frankenmuth during Zehnder's Snowfest. Carla Bronner Spletzer, Irene Bronner, Willard Scott, Lorene S. Bronner, Maria Bronner Sutorik

Accordionist
Myron Floren
performs in
Frankenmuth

Paula Zahn Newscaster

Al Roker
TV Weatherman

Julia Child
Chef

Dan Rather
CBS News Anchor

The **Lennon Sisters** of the Lawrence Welk Show

Dr. Maya Angelou
Poet and author

Wally with **Motown Group The Ink Spots**

Actor **Gordon McCrae**

Singer **Kathy Mattea**

Country music singer **Faith Hill** with
Wayne Bronner

Irene and Wally with **Charlton Heston,** actor

199

Dr. and Mrs. Norman Vincent Peale
Preacher and author

Dr. and Mrs. Charles Swindoll
Pastor and author

Rick Warren
Pastor and author

**Archbishop
Desmond Tutu**
Advocate of peace

Kevin Leman
Christian Counselor

Randy Carlson
Christian Counselor

India Children's Choir

Margaret Thatcher
England's
Prime Minister

The Fabulous Hubcaps, '50s band

Wally & grandsons Garrett & Dietrich with **Victor Borge**, entertainer & pianist

Wally with **Marianne & Michael Hartl**, European Alpine TV entertainers

Carla Bronner
Bavarian Festival Princess, 1974

Sheri Rose Shepherd
1994 Mrs. USA

A Bevy of 2002 Michigan Beauties

Christopher and Maria Bronner Sutorik with **James Earl Jones**, actor

Wally and Frankenmuth's **Marv Herzog** Polka Hall of Fame Musician

Johnny Cash, singer

Anita Bryant, singer

Irene with **Andrae Crouch,** Christian musician

Cindy Williams, actress

Dale Evans, actress

Wally with **Pat Paulsen,** comedian

Dick and Tom Smothers, comedians

Garrett & Dietrich Bronner with **Christian Steinbach**, collectible German nutcracker producer

Thomas Kincaid
Artist

Early pioneers in the Christmas decoration industry (l to r): **Helmut Krebs**, who started glass ornament production in 1947; **Kurt Adler** of New York City, who started an importing business in 1946; **Wally Bronner**, who started a sign and display business in 1945 and is credited for originating the concept of a year-round Christmas store.

Greg and Lisa Wicking and sons Mason, Colt, Dalon and **BRONNER** (front center). Their visits to Bronner's influenced naming their son, who was born on Christmas Day.

Annie Fitzgerald
Dear God series artist from Ireland

Wally with **Lem Barney**, Detroit
Lions football star

Mickey Mantle, New York Yankees baseball star &
Gene Freedman founder of Enesco Giftware Corp.

Ernie Harwell
Veteran Detroit
Tigers baseball
announcer

Pat Boone
Entertainer

Tom and Marge Monaghan
Founder of Domino's Pizza and former owner
of the Detroit Tigers

Erma Bombeck
Author

Art Buchwald
Columnist

Martha Dixon
TV Hostess

Gordie & Colleen Howe
Detroit Red Wings Hockey Star

Dr. Harold
and Jeanne
Braeutigam
with **Ray
Scott**, Detroit
Pistons
basketball star

Wally with **Dr. Peter & Joanne
McPherson**, president of Michigan
State University

204

17 | Forward

Some years ago teenager Wally saw a movie with an ending caption, "The Beginning," which proved to stimulate Wally's forward thinking.

Many new books end with a conclusion. The Bronner family and team conclude that every day is a new beginning where we move forward as we welcome and respond to comments and suggestions from our many salesroom, phone, correspondence, and website guests.

Daily we are thankful for all who have served in the armed forces to protect our nation's freedoms. These "he-roes" and "she-roes" defend our freedoms of press, speech, assembly, and religion, and our right to approach the government.

A classmate of Wally's, Marie Bickel Creger, asked him to hand letter a Biblical passage on a cupboard in her home. That passage, in addition to those below, reminds Wally to be ever thankful and

joyful, and regularly seek the Lord's guidance in the Bible.

Galatians 5: 22 & 23 But the spiritual nature produces love, joy, peace, patience, kindness, goodness, faithfulness, gentleness, and self-control. There are no laws against things like that.

Philippians 4: 6 & 7 Never worry about anything. But in every situation let God know what you need in prayers and requests while giving thanks. Then God's peace, which goes beyond anything we can imagine, will guard your thoughts and emotions through Christ Jesus.

Colossians 3:17 Everything you say or do should be done in the name of the Lord Jesus, giving thanks to God the Father through him.

Revelation 3: 20 Look, I'm standing at the door and knocking. If anyone listens to my voice and opens the door, I'll come in.

daily ... the Bronner family is joyfully thankful for opportunities of the past and those that are ours every morning. We are thankful for advisors, friends, loyal and talented team members, future generations of the Bronner family and their potential involvement in the business, suppliers, the media, and an ever-growing number of guests.

Thank You...**EVERYONE**
for Past and Future Guidance

BECAUSE OF OTHERS...
WE ARE!
...AND PROCEED...
FORWARD!

...Wally is thankful for the many that have helped him

Aunt Hattie
Role Model

Wife Irene
Motivator and
Generator

Supportive parents **Ella** and **Herman**, Brother **Arnold** and sister **Helen**

Thankful for 2nd generation (and third) who carry on the tradition and are leading the business into the future. **Lorene** and **Wayne Bronner**, **Maria** and **Chris Sutorik**, **Carla** and **Bob Spletzer**

Edmund Arnold who suggested the Bavarian theme for Frankenmuth

Herb Keinath who suggested Bronner's relocate

 **...Wally and Irene and all the Bronner family think...**

Thank You!

to GOD
for all the bountiful blessings

Thank You!

to EVERY TEAM MEMBER
through the years

Thank You!

to ALL THE GUESTS
who visit in person,
via phone, mail or website

Thank You!

to ALL THE SUPPLIERS,
CONSULTANTS AND
THE MEDIA.

Dear Reader...

**Our hope is that you enjoyed reading this Picturesque Story.
You are invited to make many visits to Picturesque
Bronner's CHRISTmas Wonderland.**

A two-page description of Bronner's is available in **10
LANGUAGES:** English, Spanish, German, French, Italian, Polish,
Greek, Arabic, Japanese, and Chinese.

210

God Bless You
ENGLISH

BONIS OMNIBUS PROSEQUI DEI TE	LAI DIEVS SVĒTĪ	GODS SEEN
LATIN	LATVIAN	AFRIKAANS

DEUS O ABENÇOE	نیا یا نف	ܐܠܗܐ ܢܒܪܟܟ
PORTUGUESE	PERSIAN-FARSI	ARAMAIC
GUD VÄL SIGNE DIG	ԱՍՏՈՒԱԾ ՕՐՀՆԷ ՔԵԶ	신 의 은 총
SWEDISH	ARMENIAN	KOREAN
DIAS MUIRE DUIT	JUMALA SIUNATKOON	ᯁᯩ ᯤ᯲ ᯬᯓᯱ
GAELIC	FINNISH	SINHALISE

БОТ ЛА ВИ БЛАГОСЛОВИ	GOTT BEHÜTE DICH	MUNGU AKUBARIKI
BULGARIAN	GERMAN	SWAHILI
KAAWAAN KA NANG MAYKAPAL	Dumnezeu Să Te Aibă În Pază	ELOHIM-YESH-MI-RECHA
TAGALOG	RUMANIAN	ISRAELI
DIEVE PADĖK	TUHAN BESERTAMU	BOG VAS BLAGOSLOVI
LITHUANIAN	INDONESIAN	SLOVANIC

主佑您	بارك الله فيك	תְּבָרֶךָ בְּרָדָר	NIECH BÓG POBŁOGOSŁAWI
	ARABIC	HEBREW	POLISH
	GOTT SÄGNE DI	सप्तबानउत्तपफा सल्ला कै	CHÚA BAN ƠN ANH
CHINESE	SWISS	HINDI	VIETNAMESE
		DIGAN NIHLZ HOGLNE DÖO	FA'AMANUIA LE ATUA TA TE OE
		NAVAJO	SAMOAN

The 8-ft. mural in Bronner's salesroom was painted by Bronner staff artist
FRANK FULCO in 1978. The scene is of the Harry Anderson painting titled
"Prince of Peace." The mural was the focal point for the Bronner entry in the
1978 Bavarian Festival Parade.

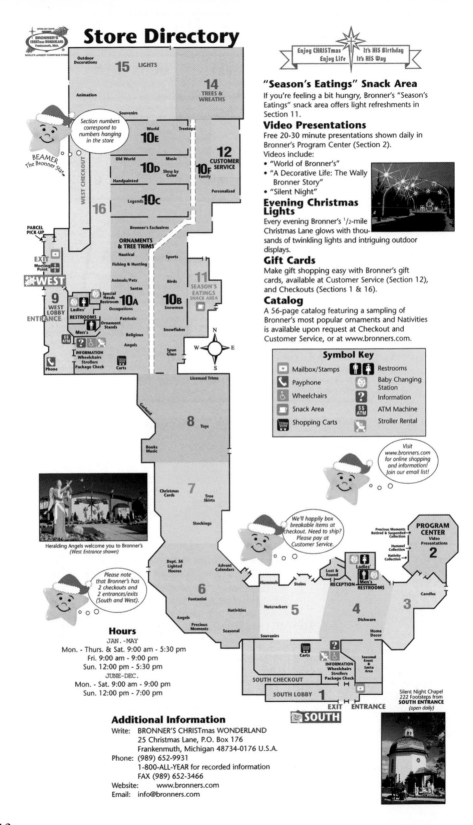

Store Directory

Enjoy CHRISTmas   It's HIS Birthday
Enjoy Life   It's HIS Way

"Season's Eatings" Snack Area

If you're feeling a bit hungry, Bronner's "Season's Eatings" snack area offers light refreshments in Section 11.

Video Presentations

Free 20-30 minute presentations shown daily in Bronner's Program Center (Section 2).
Videos include:
- "World of Bronner's"
- "A Decorative Life: The Wally Bronner Story"
- "Silent Night"

Evening Christmas Lights

Every evening Bronner's 1/2-mile Christmas Lane glows with thousands of twinkling lights and intriguing outdoor displays.

Gift Cards

Make gift shopping easy with Bronner's gift cards, available at Customer Service (Section 12), and Checkouts (Sections 1 & 16).

Catalog

A 56-page catalog featuring a sampling of Bronner's most popular ornaments and Nativities is available upon request at Checkout and Customer Service, or at www.bronners.com.

Symbol Key

Mailbox/Stamps		Restrooms	
Payphone		Baby Changing Station	
Wheelchairs		Information	
Snack Area		ATM Machine	
Shopping Carts		Stroller Rental	

Visit www.bronners.com for online shopping and information! Join our email list!

We'll happily box breakable items at checkout. Need to ship? Please pay at Customer Service.

Section numbers correspond to numbers hanging in the store.

Please note that Bronner's has 2 checkouts and 2 entrances/exits (South and West).

Heralding Angels welcome you to Bronner's (West Entrance shown)

Silent Night Chapel 222 Footsteps from SOUTH ENTRANCE (open daily)

Hours

JAN.-MAY
Mon. - Thurs. & Sat. 9:00 am - 5:30 pm
Fri. 9:00 am - 9:00 pm
Sun. 12:00 pm - 5:30 pm
JUNE-DEC.
Mon. - Sat. 9:00 am - 9:00 pm
Sun. 12:00 pm - 7:00 pm

Additional Information

Write: BRONNER'S CHRISTmas WONDERLAND
25 Christmas Lane, P.O. Box 176
Frankenmuth, Michigan 48734-0176 U.S.A.
Phone: (989) 652-9931
1-800-ALL-YEAR for recorded information
FAX (989) 652-3466
Website: www.bronners.com
Email: info@bronners.com

Appendix

The appendix contains
some duplicate information
from the
**PICTURESQUE
STORY
OF
BRONNER'S
CHRISTmas WONDERLAND**

The various details are a record
of facts, dates, statistics,
and happenings during
the first 60 years of the
Bronner family business
established in 1945.

The information may also
be a helpful reference
to answer questions such as...

"Who?   What?   When?

Where?   Why?"

ORGANIZATIONAL CHART

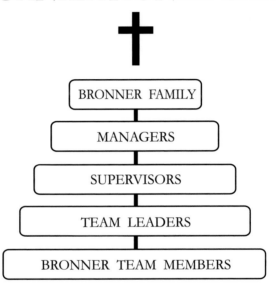

The Bronner family feels that every team member
is a leader rather than a boss. Leaders lead themselves
with their minds and lead others with their hearts. The
boss for our family is our Lord. Throughout each day we
attempt to guide the business in a Lord-pleasing manner.

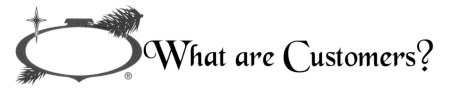

What are Customers?

Customers are very important people to Bronner's...in person, on the phone, on the internet, through e-mail & correspondence.

Customers are not dependent on us, we are dependent on them.

Customers are not an interruption of our work; they are the purpose of it. We are not doing them a favor by serving them; they are doing us a favor by giving us the opportunity.

Customers are not outsiders to our business; they are the most vital part of it.

Customers are not cold statistics–names & addresses in a computer or on invoices. They are flesh & blood human beings with feelings and emotions like our own.

Customers may not always be right, but they are always customers.

Customers are always welcomed visitors and should be treated as special guests.

Customers are people who bring us their wants. It's our challenge to serve them cheerfully and equitably so they will return to enjoy **Bronner's CHRISTmas Wonderland** again, again, again, and again.

> **"What are Customers?"**
> **is a daily reminder to the Bronner Staff.**

Bronner Team Tree

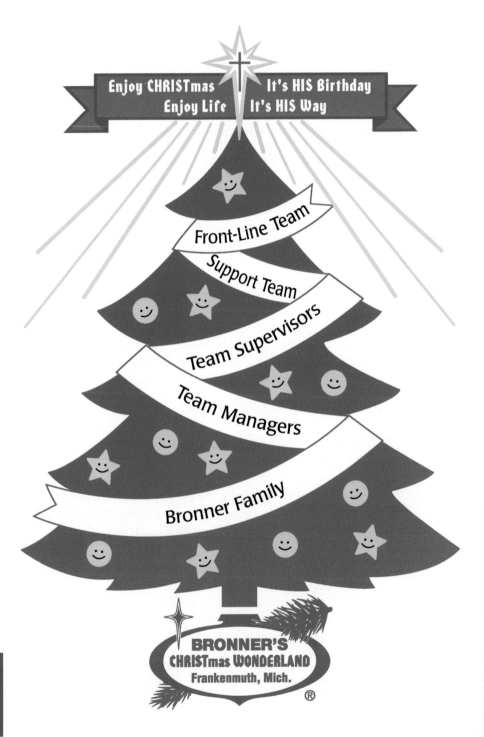

Enjoy CHRISTmas   It's HIS Birthday
Enjoy Life   It's HIS Way

Front-Line Team

Support Team

Team Supervisors

Team Managers

Bronner Family

BRONNER'S
CHRISTmas WONDERLAND
Frankenmuth, Mich.

Happy Guests Are Bronner's Most Cherished Ornaments

The Bronner team's zeal, zip, and zest is doing what's BEST for the GUEST.

The Happy Face Tree illustrates that making guests happy is the #1 priority of this business. Without guests and resulting sales, a business cannot exist. It is important that we make each of our guests happy. Each member of the Bronner staff should be a positive encourager. Let's encourage each other to be positive, which results in happiness and the feeling of a job well done.

Word-of-mouth recommendation is the most common way that our guests hear about Bronner's. Approximately 60 percent of our visitors tell us on visitor comment forms that they first heard about Bronner's from a friend or relative. If our guests go away happy, they will go home and tell their friends and family about Bronner's. This creates new guests and maintains loyal visitors.

The result of making guests happy should be truly satisfied visitors and a good feeling for each staff member. In the competitive world, what once might have been considered extraordinary customer service has now become the expected standard.

In the spirit of Frankenmuth gemütlichkeit (hospitality), let's make it our #1 goal to treat Bronner's guests as we would treat guests in our own homes: with a constant spirit of "open house." Let's continuously host our guests with #1 attention by a #1 friendly staff in a #1 store with #1 style ... and all of that in a Lord-pleasing manner. All of the Bronner family members want to be of #1 assistance so that our entire #1 Bronner team can continue to be known as a group that strives for exemplary customer service.

The smiling ornaments represent Bronner's happy guests. It takes the combined efforts of our entire team to make our guests happy. Those who have the most impact on making guests happy are the frontline team members who deal directly with the guests - either in person or via the phone, mail, or website. Those who work behind-the-scenes also have a very important role in making sure that everything is operating efficiently and smoothly to service guests. It takes the combined efforts of the frontline and support team, the team supervisors, team managers, and the Bronner family to make our guests happy and to keep them happy.

The team spirit of our staff is expressed by the ribbon wrapping through the tree. The treetop is Bronner's motto. The Star of Bethlehem radiates the spirit of the season year 'round. The base of the tree is Bronner's logo.

Bronner Buildings
Through the Decades

Throughout Bronner's first 60 years of business, over 30 locations were occupied for designing and constructing signs and displays; operating the screen printing business; and storing, displaying, and selling Christmas decorations. The following is a listing of various locations and time periods:

1940s **Basement of parents' home**
290 Haas Street

Storage garage
100 block Haas Street

Roth Carpentry Shop
113 E. Tuscola Street

Hubinger Grocery – 2nd floor
113 E. Tuscola Street

Hubinger Grocery – basement
113. E. Tuscola Street

1950s **Former two-room school building**
400 block E. Genesee Street

First permanent building (Bronner's Christmas Decorations & Bronner Displays and Signs)
121 E. Tuscola Street

Star of the West warehouse (storage in corner of warehouse)
100 block E. Tuscola Street

Welding shop building
100 block E. Tuscola Street

Chicken coop
100 block E. Tuscola Street

Storage shed
100 block E. Tuscola Street

Building in Hubinger Grove
600 block E. Tuscola Street

1960s **Ken Theatre**
195 E. Jefferson Street

Warehouse of Baker Auto Sales
616 S. Main Street

Warehouse of Frankenmuth Woolen Mill
570 S. Main Street

Weiss warehouse
200 block Walnut Street

Former Frankenmuth Bank (Bronner's Tannenbaum Shop)
NE corner Main & Tuscola Streets

Former Engel house
225 S. Main Street

Addition to permanent building
121 E. Tuscola Street

1970s **Hubinger Grocery (transformed into Bronner's Bavarian Corner)**
113 E. Tuscola Street

Semi-trailer storage (behind Engel house)
225 S. Main Street

Ron Bronner warehouse (1,600 sq. ft.)
393 List Street

All-new Bronner screen printing building
1400 Weiss Street

Ron Bronner warehouse (additional 1,120 sq. ft.)
393 List Street

Ron Bronner warehouse (additional 1,600 sq. ft.)
393 List Street

All-new CHRISTmas Wonderland
25 Christmas Lane

Ron Bronner warehouse (additional 2,680 sq. ft.)
393 List Street

1980s **Ron Bronner warehouse**
(additional 8,800 sq. ft. for 15,800 total sq. ft.)
393 List Street

1990s **Doubled size of Wonderland building**
25 Christmas Lane

Former screen-print building
(converted into Bronner's shipping department)
1400 Weiss Street

Addition to Ron Bronner warehouse (additional 9,600 sq. ft.)
305 List Street

Replica of Oberndorf, Austria, Silent Night Memorial Chapel added to 25 Christmas Lane south point of property
25 Christmas Lane

11,850 sq.-ft. Heinlein Strasse warehouse
333 Heinlein Strasse

2000s **30,000-sq.-ft. addition to Bronner's shipping department completed in 2000**
25 Christmas Lane

22,000-sq.-ft. warehouse (directly across the street from Bronner's main buildings purchased in 2002)
333 Heinlein Strasse

80,000-sq.-ft. addition to main Christmas building completed in 2002, providing a larger and more customer-friendly salesroom, a new and expanded customer service department, a larger west checkout area, and more behind-the-scenes space.
25 Christmas Lane

5,000-plus sq. ft. at south checkout renovated and 4,200 sq. ft. of space added in 2003
25 Christmas Lane

500 sq. ft. of behind-the-scenes warehouse area converted to salesroom space
25 Christmas Lane

2,100 sq. ft. of behind-the-scenes warehouse area converted to salesroom space
25 Christmas Lane

Chronology of Bronner's CHRISTmas Wonderland

1942 • Wallace "Wally" Bronner at age 15, painted his first outdoor sign, identifying St. Lorenz Tuscola District School.

1943 • Wally started painting scenic backgrounds for school plays.

1944 • More and more requests came to Wally for signs and displays, making him realize that a hobby could become a vocation.

1945 • Wally officially started a sign-painting business in his parents' basement.

• Wally enrolled in commercial courses at the Business Institute of Saginaw.

1946 • Wally lettered trucks and decorated booths at the Saginaw County Fair.

1947 • Freelance window display business increased as did fair booth decorations and exhibits.

• Wally's brother Arnold and sister, Helen Bronner Rupprecht, and friend Roland Gugel, assisted part-time.

• Wally landed his first major display account with Jennison Hardware in Bay City.

1948 • Business expanded to include interior seasonal decorations for hotels in Flint, Saginaw, and Bay City, and for the Zehnder and Fischer restaurants in Frankenmuth.

1949 • Wally hired Eddie Beyerlein as Bronner's first full-time employee.

• Wally decorated windows on a freelance, monthly basis for stores in Frankenmuth, Bay City, Saginaw, and Owosso.

1950 • The demand for outdoor signs, graphic panels, and billboards grew.

1951 • Bronner's added Christmas decorations for cities to its product line. (Bronner's first city decoration account was for Clare, Michigan.)

• Wallace Bronner married Irene Ruth Pretzer on June 23.

1952 • Bronner's displayed Christmas products in a spring showing at the Frankenmuth Township Hall and in a fall showing at St. Lorenz School gymnasium.

• Wally rented a vacant, one-room public school building to allow for year-round display of Christmas decorations.

1953 • Bronner's used the building once known as the Roth Carpentry Shop as a sign-painting area

• Bronner's issued its first four-page catalog of Bronner-produced commercial Christmas decorations.

1954 • Bronner's prepared a Christmas decorations exhibit for the Saginaw County Fair.

• Wally's father and uncle, Herman and Richard Bronner, built Bronner's first permanent building (66 ft. by 66 ft.) at 121 East Tuscola Street.

1955 • Bronner's began selling Christmas and all-seasons decorations directly to stores.

1956 • Bronner's installed their first three billboards on the north, south, and west roads leading into Frankenmuth. The billboards featured an illustration of the exterior of the salesroom.

1957 • Bronner's issued the first four-page news bulletin, "Bronner's Christmas Decorations EXTRA."

1958 • Edmund C. Arnold's article, "Christmas in the Marketplace," appeared in "This Day," magazine, giving Bronner's its first national coverage.

1959 • Bronner's display department started producing point-of-purchase displays for Michigan Bell Telephone Co. and Mountain States Telephone Co.

1960 • The entire business incorporated under the name Bronner Display and Sign Advertising, Inc. and added home decorations to the product line.

1961 • The business line expanded to include shopping center decorations. Bronner's held the first flower show in February, which featured artificial flowers and plants.

1962 • Wally Bronner served on a committee to design and produce the official city of Frankenmuth crest.

1963 • Bronner's 1954 building was doubled in size, and a second-story stockroom was added to a portion of the building.

1964 • Bronner's installed its first billboard on I-75 in Michigan, 10 miles south of exit 136, advertising Bronner's salesroom.

1965 • Wally visited trade fairs in Germany and Italy, initiating the direct import of Christmas merchandise, including glass ornaments produced from Bronner's designs in religious, traditional, and toyland themes.

- With the purchase of the first of three privately owned plots of land, the Bronners commenced the acquisition of the V-shaped lot where Bronner's buildings now stand. (The first plot purchased was a section of the Harry and Bertha Conzelmann farm.)

1966 • Bronner's purchased the vacated Frankenmuth Bank building and opened Bronner's Tannenbaum Shop.

- Bronner's bought the Engel house and rented a portion of the Baker Chevrolet salesroom for storage.

- Wally and Irene purchased the second portion of acreage for Bronner's Weiss Street site. (The second plot purchased was a section of the Herbert and Renata List farm.)

1967 • Bronner's established a personalized ornament department.

1968 • Bronner's discontinued production of large highway signs, devoting full attention to the decoration, display, and other sign business.

- The sign portion of the business moved to a building behind the Edelweiss Restaurant.

1969 • Bronner's first 40-foot-container shipment arrived from Europe.

- Bronner's patented its own fiberglass life-size Nativity molds.

- Wally and Irene purchased the third portion of acreage for Bronner's Weiss Street site. (The third plot purchased was a section of the Harold and Marcella Weber farm.)

1970 • Preliminary planning started for relocating the business from the center of Frankenmuth to the south side. Meetings were held with the city planning commission, rezoning property to accommodate the business.

1971 • Bronner's patented its Christmas and garden elves molds.

- Bronner's Bavarian Corner opened in the former Hubinger Grocery Store.

1972 • Bronner's developed a four-foot fiberglass Nativity.

1973 • Bronner's offered ornaments and Nativities at trade marts in New York, Chicago, Los Angeles, Dallas, Miami, and Atlanta.

1974 • Bronner's designed and introduced an exclusive annual ornament.

- Family coat-of-arms plaques were produced for home and business décor.

1975 • Bronner's sold the Main Store and Sign Shop, Tannenbaum Shop, Bronner's Bavarian Corner, and the Engel house to Star of the West Milling Company.

- Construction began on Bronner's new buildings on Weiss Street.

1976 • Bronner's Screen Printing building opened on Weiss Street.

• Governor Milliken designated Bronner's Christmas Decorations an embassy of Michigan tourism.

• Wally first discussed with Oberndorf, Austria, officials the possibility of erecting a replica of the Silent Night Memorial Chapel in Frankenmuth, Michigan.

• John Wayne placed a telephone order to Bronner's for a Santa suit.

1977 • Bronner's opened new Christmas salesroom at Weiss Street location on June 8.

• A community open house was held at the Bronner Screen Printing building.

• Wally reserved a landscaped spot on the south end of Bronner's property on Weiss Street for future construction of the Silent Night Memorial Chapel.

1978 • The Bronner staff constructed displayers and stockroom shelving and landscaped the new Christmas salesroom property in preparation for the first full year at the all-new location where a community open house was held on May 10 and 11.

1979 • Bronner's sent its first major export shipment to Myer's Emporium in Australia.

• Wally and Irene Bronner led the first annual Christmas Caroling Sing-along session in Bronner's program center.

• Bronner's introduced the motto, "Enjoy CHRISTmas, It's HIS birthday; Enjoy Life, It's HIS way."

1980 • Bronner's held its first annual Goebel Hummel Days.

• Bronner Screen Printing incorporated as a separate business, a subsidiary of Bronner Display and Sign Advertising, Inc., with Don Fischer as corporation president and general manager and Bob Reindel as vice president and director of sales.

• Bronner's started advertising on billboards on I-75 near Ocala, Florida, north of Disney World, and at the interchange of the Pennsylvania and Ohio Turnpikes.

1981 • Bronner's joined Circle Michigan, an organization promoting tour group travel to Michigan.

• Wally and Irene appointed daughter Carla assistant general manager at Bronner's.

- Bronner's introduced a profit-sharing plan for its employees.

1982 • Bronner's constructed a 350-car parking lot on the west side of the building and added a 1,600-foot driveway (25 Christmas Lane), which provided an entrance to Bronner's from Main Street.

- Bronner's received the Retailer of the Year Award presented by the National Ornament and Electric Lights Christmas Association (NOEL).

- AAA named Frankenmuth Michigan's #1 Tourist Attraction.

1983 • Bronner's held its first annual Precious Moments Days with originator Sam Butcher and associate Bill Biel present.

- Son Wayne joined the Bronner staff as assistant general manager, and his wife Lorene also joined the management team.

- A computer and word processor were installed.

- The "World of Bronner's," an 18-minute, 10-projector, multi-image presentation, was developed for showing in Bronner's program center.

1984 • The first edition of Bronner's "Staff Tidings," a monthly, employee newsletter, was published.

- The "World of Bronner's" 10-projector presentation began scheduled showings to the public.

- Bronner's installed a 1-800-ALL-YEAR number for recorded hours information in Michigan.

- The Bronner Screen Printing/Memtron Technologies business was sold to long-time manager Don Fischer and his wife Karen.

1985 • Bronner's celebrated its 40th year in business.

- Christmas Lane began to be illuminated every evening from dusk to midnight.

- Sam Butcher, Precious Moments artist, lectured and signed during Bronner's Precious Moments Days.

- Todd Spence, producer of the "World of Bronner's" multi-image presentation, received the Addy Award of Excellence.

- AAA of Michigan listed Bronner's as one of the "Top 10 Man-made Attractions in Michigan."

- Bronner's began using the name "Bronner's CHRISTmas Wonderland" in its business logo and advertisements.

1986 • Bronner's converted from a mainframe computer system to a networking system on personal computers.

- Bronner's received the first Golden Santa Claus Award presented at the Nuremberg International Toy Fair.
- Bronner buyers visited trade fairs in Czechoslovakia and Leipzig, Germany.

1987
- As of January, 300,000 guests had viewed the "World of Bronner's."
- Wally received the Master Entrepreneur Award from Saginaw Valley State University.

1988
- Bronner's began painting their life-size Nativity figures on location in Frankenmuth.
- Wally Bronner formally requested permission from Dr. Raimund Traintinger, Mayor of Oberndorf, Austria, to erect a replica of the Austrian Silent Night Memorial Chapel at Bronner's CHRISTmas Wonderland in Frankenmuth.
- Bronner's produced "Bronner's Christmas Favorites" ornament and Nativities catalog for consumers and dealers.
- Bronner's began using the phrase "World's Largest Christmas Store" in its logo.
- Bronner's information sheet became available in the English, German, Italian, French, and Spanish languages. In 1992 Bronner's added Japanese, in 1994 they added Chinese and Arabic, and in 1995 Bronner's added Greek and Polish.
- Son-in-law Bob Spletzer, Carla's husband, joined the management team at Bronner's.
- Bronner's advertised on 78 billboards in five states.

1989
- By late June, 500,000 had viewed the "World of Bronner's" since its premiere five years earlier.
- In November the City and Visitors' Bureau of Oberndorf, Austria, granted Bronner's permission to replicate the Austrian Silent Night Memorial Chapel in Frankenmuth, Michigan.
- Daughter Maria Bronner Sutorik joined the Bronner management team.
- Bronner's began the final planning process and engaged an architect and general contractor for a $6 million (95,500 square-foot) expansion of the salesroom and stockroom. Ground was broken and footings were poured in late fall.

- Construction workers converted 5,000 square feet of warehouse space to salesroom space to connect the existing salesroom with the new expansion.
- Bronner's produced the "Bronner's CHRISTmas Wonderland" video for sale and offered it in both a VHS format and European PAL version.

1990
- Bronner's completed its currency display featuring one low denomination of paper currency from every nation in the world.
- An additional 5,000 square feet of salesroom opened in June.
- Bronner's first 40-foot container from the Orient arrived.
- Building contractor and cousin Ron Bronner visited Oberndorf, Austria, with Wally to make building sketches of the Silent Night Chapel.
- The Bronner business moved into portions of the new 95,500 square-foot building that doubled the size of the complex.
- "People" magazine featured Wally Bronner and Bronner's.

1991
- A patriotic tree in the Bronner salesroom displayed photos of staff family members serving in Operation Desert Storm.
- Bronner's new Season's Eatings snack area and salesroom expansion opened to the public on May 23.
- Construction began on a corridor to connect the Christmas building with the north building.
- The shipping and ornament-lettering departments moved into the 18,000 square-foot north building (formerly Memtron).
- Bronner's added 263 car spaces and 14 bus spots to the parking lot.
- ABC'S "Home Show" filmed at Bronner's with "Christmas Corner" hostess Carol Duvall.
- "CBS This Morning" filmed live at Bronner's, with Wally and Irene Bronner interviewed via satellite by Paula Zahn.

1992
- Bronner's held expansion open houses for the Frankenmuth chamber members, business associates, and the Frankenmuth community. (Special guests at the business open house included Michigan's Governor John Engler and his wife Michelle.)
- Bronner's broke ground early in the year for the construction of the Silent Night Memorial Chapel.
- The American School of Needlework published "Santas at Work and Play," a cross-stitch booklet with artwork by Connie Larsen, Bronner's staff artist.

- Bronner's dedicated its Silent Night Memorial Chapel replica on November 20. Raimund Traintinger and his family (former mayor of Oberndorf, Austria) and Volker and Norbert Wratschko (ornament suppliers) participated in the dedication ceremonies for the media and Frankenmuth public.

1993
- As of June, 750,000 guests had viewed the "World of Bronner's."
- Wally Bronner traveled to the University of Salzburg in Austria, (by invitation) to speak in a symposium commemorating the 175th anniversary of the beloved hymn "Silent Night."
- The Bronner staff collected a verse of "Silent Night" in 175 languages to present to the Austrians at the symposium and to display on the grounds of Bronner's chapel.
- AAA-Chicago Motor Club recognized Bronner's CHRISTmas Wonderland as a "Travel Treasure" in their November/December issue of "Home & Away" travel magazine.
- Bronner's mailed its retail catalog, "Bronner's Christmas Favorites," to thousands of homes cross the country and around the world.
- Bronner's became a smoke-free establishment.

1994
- Wally and Irene Bronner accompanied Jimmy Thompson of Caffco Corporation for tours to their factories in Pacific Rim Nations.
- Bronner's held its first Department 56 Village Gathering, hosting Jeanne-Marie Dickens, founder of the Charles Dickens Heritage Foundation and wife of Christopher Dickens, great-great-grandson of Charles Dickens.
- Bronner buyers Wally Bronner, Anne Koehler, and Doris Reda made their first major buying trip to the Orient.
- Bronner's produced a video of the Silent Night Chapel.
- Staff member Eddie Beyerlein retired after 46 years. He and his wife Jane continue to produce wooden stables for Bronner's.
- Carol Duvall of "Our Home" talk show filmed two segments at Bronner's. The segments aired nationwide on Lifetime cable television.
- Bronner's introduced a tabletop, ceramic, illuminated, musical Bronner's Silent Night Chapel simulating Oberndorf, Austria's Silent Night Chapel.
- Hanno Schilf, author and film producer of Salzburg, Austria, premiered the English version of his book "Silent Night, Holy Night," at Bronner's, with an Austrian National Television team present.

- Bronner's pictorial souvenir book was produced for sale and promotional use.

1995 • Bronner's commemorated its 50th year.

- St. Lorenz Lutheran Church and Frankenmuth commemorated their 150th anniversaries.

- Wally Bronner received the NOEL Hall of Fame award in New York City.

- "Selling Christmas Decorations" and "Gifts & Decorative Accessories" trade publications featured Bronner's 50th year.

- Wally Bronner received the appointment of delegate to the first-ever White House Conference on Tourism where he met President Clinton.

- Son-in-law Christopher Sutorik, husband of Maria, joined the Bronner team as visual merchandising manager.

- Bronner's hosted a 50th anniversary reception for Frankenmuth, Saginaw, Bridgeport, and Birch Run Chambers of Commerce and business associates.

- Three Hummel artists appeared at Hummel Days in honor of Bronner's 50th year.

- Ernst & Young honored Wally as Michigan Master Entrepreneur of the Year.

- Mayor Andreas Kinzl and wife Rosa of Oberndorf, Austria, visited Bronner's Silent Night Memorial Chapel replica.

- Glassblowers Thomas and Marlene Horn from Lauscha, Germany, made two appearances at Bronner's.

- Bronner's held its first "Meet Originator Wally Bronner" autograph sessions.

- The "Saginaw News" published a special edition section for Bronner's 50th year.

- CNN and "Good Morning America" both filmed holiday segments at Bronner's.

- Dollywood Theme Park began purchasing decorations from Bronner's.

1996 • Wally Bronner presented Frankenmuth pretzel Valentines to Paula Zahn, Harry Smith, Jane Robelot, and Mark McEwen during the "CBS This Morning" broadcast on February 14.

- "Good Morning America" photojournalist Linda Solomon completed a photo shoot at Bronner's and Frankenmuth.

- Bronner's parking lot expansion added 300 more spaces, allowing Bronner's lots to accommodate a total of 1,200 guest vehicles.
- Bronner's commercial department began selling Christmas decorations to movie sets with its initial sale to "Jingle All the Way."
- Bronner's presented President Bill Clinton, Vice-President Al Gore, presidential candidate Bob Dole, and vice-presidential candidate Jack Kemp with personalized ornaments during conferences and political meetings.
- The Department 56 musical Silent Night Chapel premiered at Bronner's in the spring.
- The "Saginaw News" earned first place in the 1996 Newspaper Association of America Award for Excellence for the 24-page tabloid they produced in 1995 for Bronner's 50th anniversary.
- Christian and Gunther Ulbricht, leading nutcracker producers from the Erzgebirge region of Germany, were popular with guests and staff during a signing event at Bronner's in June.
- Woodcarver Eddie Walker of Midwest of Cannon Falls, doll artist Chuck Thorndike, Disney sculptor Patrick Simmons, and Disney Manager of Special Events Shar Bullock visited Bronner's in 1996 for signing events.
- Bronner's Orna-Pak™, the plastic boxes exclusively designed for packaging Bronner's 8-cm. and 10-cm. Austrian ornaments, were introduced.
- Don Fenton, vice-president of sales for Fenton Art Glass, and Emanuele Fontanini, fourth-generation member of the Italian family of Nativity producers, visited Bronner's for signing events.
- Wally and Irene Bronner received the 1996 Frank N. Andersen Spirit of Philanthropy Award. The crystal award is presented to individuals who have a history of outstanding leadership and who demonstrate an extraordinary commitment to improving the quality of life in Saginaw County.
- Candace Miller, Michigan secretary of state, chose Wally Bronner to be one of nine judges who selected the artwork of 12 semifinalists for a new license plate design in the Great State Plate Challenge.
- Wally and Irene Bronner celebrated their 45th wedding anniversary.
- Stumpy the Talking Tree debuted at Bronner's.

- Wally Bronner served as honorary chairman for the American Cancer Society's 1996 Holiday Greeting Card Campaign.

- Department 56 introduced a collectible Silent Night Chapel at Bronner's.

- In September, Bronner's made the leap into cyberspace with the introduction of a website on the Internet at www.bronners.com.

- "Bronner's Christmas Favorites" 1996-1997 catalog grew, offering a full 48 pages of Christmas treasures. A total of 500,000 catalogs were mailed to arrive in homes just in time for holiday shopping.

- Mesh shopping bags were introduced as a new option for customers.

- The grandson of the originator of Raggedy Ann and Andy purchased Raggedy Ann ornaments from Bronner's.

- Polka king Marv Herzog celebrated 50 years in the music profession during his annual Christmas sing-along at Bronner's.

1997 • Bronner's CHRISTmas Wonderland became one of only four national winners of the 1997 Blue Chip Enterprise Initiative Award. The award, presented to Bronner's in Washington, D.C., is sponsored by the U.S. Chamber of Commerce and Mass Mutual, and recognizes successful businesses that have overcome small-business challenges.

- Wally gave a speech of tribute to glass Christmas ornament producers in Lauscha, Germany, as part of the 150th anniversary celebration of glass Christmas ornament production. The art originated in Lauscha in 1847.

- Buick CEO Bob Coletta filmed his "Curbside Chat" for Buick dealers nationwide at Bronner's.

- NBC Today Show's Mike Leonard filmed at Bronner's in November to prepare a feature scheduled to air on December 25, 1997.

- Deacon Bernie Marquis shared "How St. Nicholas Became Santa Claus" during his December visit.

- The 700 Club's reporter/producer Gorman Woodfin filmed at Bronner's in September for a December air date with Pat Robertson.

- Santa helpers from around the world visited Bronner's during their three-day training session in October at the Charles W. Howard Santa School held in Midland, Michigan.

- Wally and Irene traveled to Gunzenhausen, Germany, to celebrate the 35-year anniversary of Gunzenhausen and Frankenmuth's sister city relationship through the People to People program.

- Bronner's was named the Goebel Retailer of the Year for the Midwest Region.
- Silver Dollar City, sister theme park to Dollywood, began purchasing decorations from Bronner's in 1997.
- Master sculptor Gerhard Skrobek of Germany demonstrated his skill and signed figurines during Bronner's Hummel Days in October.
- Alexander Goebel, sixth-generation family member of the fine giftware company in Germany, visited Bronner's in November.
- "Silent Night" in 275 languages was presented to officials of Oberndorf, Austria, during Wally and Irene's September visit.
- The Saginaw City Rescue Mission presented Wally with the Friend of the Friendless Award "for using his resources and influence to minister and provide for the homeless and needy."
- The All Area Arts Award was presented to Wally and Irene Bronner in May by the Saginaw Community Enrichment Commission. The award recognizes those who have made a significant contribution to the quality of life in Saginaw County.
- Phyllis Wallace of the Lutheran Hour Ministries' "Woman to Woman" radio talk show interviewed Wally.
- The shipping department set a new record when they shipped over 1,200 packages in one day.
- Roofing projects over the west lobby and the north building were completed.
- In April, Carol Duvall filmed segments at Bronner's for her Christmas shows which aired in December.

1998
- Originator Wally Bronner and wife Irene transferred leadership of the family business to the second generation. Son Wayne became president and CEO, and his wife Lorene continued serving as salesroom manager. Daughter Carla was appointed vice president in charge of advertising and office functions. Her husband, Bob Spletzer, remained human resource and building operations director. Daughter Maria became vice president in charge of marketing and promotions; and her husband, Christopher Sutorik, continued serving as visual and internet merchandising and display director. Wally, chairman of the board, and Irene, member of the board, remain active in the business.
- Gordie and Colleen Howe visited Bronner's to personalize copies of the Howe family biography "and . . .Howe!"

- Bronner's produced its first, exclusive wholesale catalog.
- Over 1,000 guests toured the 20th Anniversary Precious Moments Care-A-Van during its one-day stop at Bronner's in June.
- Bavarian Television and Radio from Nuremberg, Germany, interviewed Wally for a video feature.
- Wally Bronner received an honorary doctor of letters degree from Great Lakes College, which became Davenport University.
- Bronner's was named 1997 Goebel National Retailer of the Year.
- In December country singer Wynonna Judd placed a catalog phone order with Bronner's.
- Daimler-Chrysler Corporation featured Wally and a guest in Germany in a corporate holiday video about Christmas customs in the USA and Germany.
- Three British television crews taped holiday programming at Bronner's including a segment for "Good Morning Britain."
- "Michigan Magazine" videotaped a holiday program at Bronner's for airing in December.
- Tri-State Christian TV taped holiday segments on Bronner's and the Silent Night Chapel for airing in December.

1999
- Texas First Lady Laura Bush visited Bronner's in November during a campaign stop for husband George W. Bush, presidential candidate.
- Bronner's significantly expanded its online offerings.
- A new Bronner video was produced for sale. (It was the first to feature the expansion and the Silent Night Chapel.)
- Beamer the Bronner Star was developed as a mascot in conjunction with a new Bronner video "Christmas Dreams Come True."
- Bronner's converted to a new computer system.
- Wally Bronner received the Laureates Award from Junior Achievement of Northeast Michigan.
- Wally was a guest on a Silent Night documentary produced by the British Broadcast Corporation.
- "Bronner's Christmas Favorites" catalog was mailed to 1,500,000 homes in time for the 1999 holiday season.

2000
- Bronner's commemorated its 55th year in business.
- The 37,000-square-foot expansion to Bronner's shipping department opened in mid-September.

- Wally and Irene Bronner received the first annual Wally and Irene Bronner Muscular Dystrophy Association Spirit of Sharing Award.

- Film stars Mahima Chaudary and Manoj Bajpi from India taped a movie scene at Bronner's.

- Christian Goebel (M.I. Hummel), Gaylord Ho (Seraphim angels), Christian Steinbach (Steinbach nutcrackers), Gene Freedman (Precious Moments), and Stefano Fontanini (Fontanini Nativities) appeared for collectible signing events.

- Soloist Elizabeth von Trapp performed at Bronner's.

- Dell Vaughn of PBS's "Michigan Magazine" taped a program featuring author Colleen Monroe and illustrator Michael Monroe at Bronner's.

2001
- Originators Wally and Irene Bronner celebrated their 50th wedding anniversary.

- "America's Master Handyman," Glenn Haege, interviewed Wally Bronner for Haege's nationally syndicated radio program.

- Videographer Takeshi Watanabe and director Ayumi Yamato of the Shikoku Broadcasting Co., Ltd. of Tokushima, Japan, videotaped at Bronner's.

- Master painter Ulrich Tendera (M.I. Hummel), and Marco Fontanini (Fontanini Nativities) appeared for collectible signing events.

- Wally Bronner received the Impact in Ministry Award from Stephen Strang of Strang Communications.

- Radio City Rockettes, Cari Vokal and Callie Carter, appeared at Bronner's.

2002
- Bronner's 80,000-square-foot expansion opened to the public in May, making the salesroom 50 percent larger. Lieutenant Governor Dick Posthumus gave a congratulatory address during the expansion open house.

- Wally Bronner received the Christus Vivit Award from Concordia Seminary in St. Louis, Missouri.

- Davenport University presented its first annual Wally Bronner Excellence in Business Award to Wally Bronner.

- Gaylord Ho (Seraphim angels), Gene Freedman (Precious Moments), and Kristi Jensen Pierro (Snowbabies/Department 56) appeared for collectible signing events.

- Wally and Irene Bronner served as Frankenmuth Bavarian Festival Parade grand marshals.

2003 • Michigan Governor Jennifer Granholm presented Wally Bronner with the first annual Michigan Tourism Outstanding Achievement Award for the advancement of travel and tourism.

• Matt Fox and Shari Hiller from HGTV's "Room by Room" shopped at Bronner's for decorations for their 2003 holiday decorating special.

• Bronner's south entrance and checkout expansion opened to the public on June 8, 2003. The 4,000-sq.-ft. expansion included an all-new, 1,200-sq.-ft. Santa area where Santa visits with children during the holiday season.

• Ernie Harwell served as the grand marshal of Frankenmuth's annual Bavarian Festival Parade and greeted guests and signed his products purchased at Bronner's.

• Scott Enter (Department 56), Shuhei Fujioka (Precious Moments), and Alessandro Fontanini (Fontanini Nativities) appeared for collectible signing events.

• A snow machine began producing flurries in Bronner's west entrance in September.

2004 • HGTV's "Food Finds" filmed at Bronner's for their holiday special.

• Christina Goihl (M.I. Hummel) and Paul Lundberg (Department 56) attended special collectible events at Bronner's.

• Bronner's published "Ornament Legends, Symbols, & Traditions," a full-color book of 75 ornament legends, symbols, and traditions illustrated by artist Connie Larsen.

• Bronner's became the exclusive, national 2004 retailer for Laser Light ornaments.

• Wally received the Robert H. Albert Community Service Award, Saginaw County Chamber of Commerce's most prestigious honor.

• The Bronner family and staff gathered photos and data for a book entitled "The Picturesque Story of Bronner's CHRISTmas Wonderland," to be released in 2005 during Bronner's 60th year in business.

• Bronner's mailed 2.6 million "Bronner's Christmas Favorites" catalogs across the country.

• Bronner's buyers made a buying trip to China.

• Department 56 introduced an exclusive collectible building reminiscent of Bronner's Tannenbaum Shop on Main Street.

2005 • Bronner's business celebrated its 60th anniversary.

- A remodeling project added 2,100 sq. ft. to the salesroom by converting behind-the-scenes space.

- Bronner's supplied Christmas ornaments for ABC-TV's "Extreme Makeover: Wedding Edition," which aired on May 9.

- "Bronner's Christmas Favorites" catalog circulated to 3,000,000 homes for the holiday season.

- Bronner's introduced "Bronner's Flavorful Favorites" cookbook featuring over 400 recipes submitted by the Bronner team.

The popular 3-ring loose-leaf Bronner cookbook has a padded cover (7" x 9.25") and over 400 recipes shared by Bronner team members. Appetizers, tasty sides, main dishes, and desserts are featured.

12 Most Asked Questions
of Originators
Wally and Irene Bronner & Family

1. **What is BRONNER'S CHRISTmas WONDERLAND?**

Bronner's business started 60 years ago when Wally, then a senior in high school, began doing sign and display work. Since its humble beginning in 1945, Bronner's has continued to grow to keep up with requests from guests. Today, Bronner's is frequented by over 2 million visitors annually. Bronner's is the world's largest Christmas store, carrying over 50,000 gifts and trims from around the world. Animated figurines, decorated trees with thousands of ornaments and light displays all make up this wonderland. (A description of Bronner's is available in English, German, Spanish, Italian, French, Japanese, Arabic, Greek, Chinese and Polish.)

At Bronner's, guests are the lifeblood of the business. In the spirit of "Open House," we make it our goal to host our guests with #1 attention from a #1 staff in a #1 store with #1 merchandise displayed and stocked in a #1 way . . . and all of this will hopefully please the ultimate #1 - - the good Lord.

Bronner's is located on 25 Christmas Lane at the south entrance to Frankenmuth, "Michigan's Little Bavaria." Learn more about Bronner's by watching the 20-minute, digital video presentation, "World of Bronner's." Bronner's Program Center features daily showings of this presentation, which gives a detailed history of Bronner's. In addition to "World of Bronner's," the Program Center also has daily showings of "A Decorative Life: The Wally Bronner Story" and "Silent Night."

2. **What makes BRONNER'S CHRISTmas WONDERLAND the world's largest Christmas store?**

Bronner's features trims and gifts for all seasons, reasons and budgets. Over 500 styles of Nativity scenes are available, including Bronner's exclusive life-size Nativity. Six thousand styles of glass ornaments are showcased, many of which are Bronner's exclusive designs. Decorations and gifts from 70 nations are displayed. Bibles are available in 20 languages. Commercial displays are also featured for buildings, city streets, parks, and shopping malls. In addition to the store, Bronner's has a wholesale division that sells decorations to nearly 1,000 other stores. Bronner's also has a catalog and website and maintains an extensive mail order department.

3. **What is the size of BRONNER'S CHRISTmas WONDERLAND?**
Bronner's is the world's largest Christmas store, located on a 45-acre tract (18 hectares). The building, parking lot, and beautiful landscaping cover 27 acres (10.8 hectares). The building area under roof equals 320,000 square feet (5½ football fields), with the additional 48,000 square feet offsite storage bringing the total to over 1/3 million square feet (34,235 square meters, 6.4 football fields, 3.4 hectares, or 8.45 acres). Bronner's parking lot accommodates 1,250 cars and 50 motorcoaches with snowflake designs indicating the parking spots. Over 100,000 lights illuminate Bronner's ½-mile Christmas Lane every evening starting at dusk.

4. **Do you ever get tired of Christmas after being in the decorations business all year long?**
Since we anticipate its arrival all year, Christmas is very special to everyone at Bronner's. We try to make sure that the real meaning of CHRISTmas is never forgotten. Christmas at Bronner's is rehearsed all year, therefore, it is sure to be a joyous event.

5. **Why is there a replica of the Oberndorf, Austria, Silent Night Memorial Chapel at Bronner's in Frankenmuth, Michigan?**
The Silent Night Memorial Chapel is a tribute to God from Wally and Irene Bronner and Family. The original Silent Night Memorial Chapel is in Oberndorf, Austria, near Salzburg. It is on the altar site of the original St. Nicholas church in which "Stille Nacht" ("Silent Night"), composed by Joseph

Mohr and Franz Xaver Gruber, was first sung on Christmas Eve in 1818. The concept for a replica of the original Silent Night Memorial Chapel was in the developmental stages since Wally Bronner visited Oberndorf, Austria, in 1976. The City government and the Visitors' Bureau of Oberndorf granted the Bronner family permission to simulate the original Silent Night Memorial Chapel. Construction began in May 1992. The memorial was dedicated on November 20, 1992. Wally Bronner was a speaker at the 175th anniversary

"Silent Night" symposium held at the University of Salzburg, Austria, in 1993, and at the Joseph Mohr Symposium in Wagrain, Austria, in 1999.

Plaques with the hymn "Silent Night" in over 300 languages line the walkway of Bronner's chapel. Inside, visitors can view the chancel area and altar. The interior of the chapel has been decorated much like the original chapel. The memorial chapel is open daily for visitation and meditation. It is not intended for services or ceremonies.

In celebration of our Savior's birth, every year on December 24 from 3-3:15 p.m., Wally Bronner and a guest guitarist lead visitors in singing "Silent Night" at the chapel.

6. **Why does Bronner's search the world for Christmas ornaments and Nativity scenes?**
    Christmas is a joyous event and many around the world decorate to observe the birthday of Christ the Savior. A global array of unique selections is available. We hope to be able to please anyone from anywhere by providing a large assortment that is not widely available elsewhere. We also want to inform and educate people about the Christmas traditions of various nations.

7. **Why did Bronner's start designing Christmas ornaments?**
    During our travels, we discovered countless beautiful, artistic ornaments. Very few had a theme that graphically gave recognition to the true meaning of CHRISTmas. We decided to design our own. Through the years, our line continued to grow. Our 6,000 styles of ornaments include the themes of religious, traditional, toyland, commemorative, hobby and vocation. Our ornament design team continues to come up with new designs every year. We have been very successful with our past designs and look forward to the future. Approximately half of the ornaments we sell each year are our own designs. (Glass ornaments originated in Lauscha, Germany, in 1847. Wally was a speaker for the 150th Anniversary in 1997.)

8. **Why did Bronner's start producing life-size Nativity sets?**
    In America, it is difficult to find life-size Nativity sets. Some factories have discontinued production altogether. Realizing the importance of the Nativity, Bronner's introduced the first fiberglass, mass production set on the market. Since its introduction, this set has now been shipped to all five continents. The city center in Leipzig, Germany, displayed a set one month after the Iron Curtain opened up in 1989. Berlin also ordered a set one Christmas season later.

9. **Does Bronner's have a catalog? Website?**

Yes, Bronner's Christmas Favorites catalog features a selection from some of our most popular items. Highlighted in our catalog are a wide variety of unique glass ornaments including mouth-blown glass figures, old-fashioned forms, ethnic designs, and ornaments with hand-painted scenes. Also featured are exquisite Nativities, lighted outdoor silhouettes, and decorative gifts. You may order all year from Bronner's Christmas Favorites. To obtain your copy, call our toll-free catalog number, 1-800-361-6736. Visit Bronner's website, www.bronners.com, for Bronner's information and online shopping or to request our catalog and sign up for Bronner's Enewsletter.

10. **From how many nations does Bronner's import Christmas ornaments?**

Bronner's became very active in ornament designing and importing in the 1950's. Volume, variety, production and distribution increase every year. Currently, our ornaments come from the following nations - North America: USA, Mexico, Canada; Central American Nations; Europe: Germany, Austria, Italy, Czech Republic, Slovak Republic, Ukraine, Poland, Romania, Switzerland, Hungary, France, Finland, Sweden, Spain and Russia; Asia: Israel, India, Philippines, Taiwan, China, Japan and Hong Kong; Africa: Egypt; South America: Colombia, Brazil, Venezuela and Uruguay.

11. **How many people does Bronner's employ? How many people make up the Bronner Family?**

In peak season, Bronner's employs over 500 staff members. Each team member is a blessing. Wally and Irene have four children. Three of their children are married, making a total of seven. Of the seven, six are in management at Bronner's. Currently, there are five grandsons. Two already work at Bronner's part-time. The staff and family work together to assure that every visitor is satisfied.

12. **When will Wally retire?**

In Wally's case, he started with a hobby, stuck with it, and never went to work. Who retires from a hobby? In 1998, however, Wally and Irene transferred leadership of the business to the second generation. The couple plan to continue to play active roles in the business and look forward to the continuing joy of experiencing daily family reunions. Wally often comments that he is in the store most every day that ends in "y" and is thankful for every guest.

Wally - Originator, Chairman of the Board of Directors
Irene - Member of Board of Directors and active in the business
Wayne - President and CEO
Lorene (Wayne's wife) - Salesroom Manager
Carla - Vice President
Bob (Carla's husband) - Human Resource and Building Manager
Maria - Vice President
Chris (Maria's husband) - Visual & Internet Merchandising Manager

Blessed CHRISTmas always.

When Christ our Savior was born...
God loved. Mary pondered.   Joseph believed.
Shepherds praised.   Angels sang.
May you be blessed to do the same this CHRISTmas and every day.
God's continued blessings daily . . . annually . . . eternally.

Bronner's Trivia

HISTORY

- Wally Bronner originated BRONNER'S CHRISTmas WONDERLAND in 1945.

- Bronner's is owned and managed by Wally and Irene Bronner along with six family members.

- Bronner's three original salesrooms were the Main Salesroom (1954), Tannenbaum Shop (1966), and Bavarian Corner (1971).

- The present Bronner building opened June 8, 1977.

- Bronner's 100,000-sq.-ft. expansion opened May 22, 1991. Bronner's 37,000-sq.-ft. shipping expansion was up and running September 2000. An 80,000-sq.-ft. expansion opened at Bronner's in May 2002, followed by the south entrance/exit expansion in June 2003.

- In 1992, with Austria's permission, Bronner's erected a replica of the Oberndorf (Salzburg), Austria, Silent Night Memorial Chapel in tribute to the Christmas hymn "Silent Night" and in thankfulness to God.

- Bronner's motto is: "Enjoy CHRISTmas, it's HIS Birthday; Enjoy LIFE, it's HIS way"

- "Beamer the Bronner star" was born in 1999.

- During Bronner's 60th year, the 254-page book "Picturesque Story of Bronner's" was published.

BUILDING & GROUNDS INFORMATION

- Bronner's is the world's largest year-round Christmas store with 2.2 acres (1.7 football fields) of salesroom.

- Beautifully landscaped grounds cover 27 acres, with 7.35 acres (5.5 football fields) of building in Bronner's entire complex.

- Three giant outdoor Santas tower 17 feet, and the lofty snowman is 15 feet.

- Bronner's parking lot accommodates 1250 cars and 50 buses.

- Bronner's electrical bill averages $900 per day.

- Approximately 100,000 lights illuminate Bronner's ½-mile long Christmas Lane every evening from dusk to midnight.

MERCHANDISE & DISPLAYS

- Bronner's features over 50,000 trims and gifts for all seasons, reasons, and budgets.

- Half of Bronner's items sell for under $10, and two-thirds sell for under $20.

- Over 500 styles of Nativity scenes are available.

- Decorations and gifts from 70 nations are displayed, and Bibles are available in numerous languages.

- Bronner artists personalize 100,000 ornaments annually.

- Approximately 50 percent of the glass ornaments sold are Bronner's own designs, handcrafted by global artisans exclusively for Bronner's.

- "Merry Christmas" ornaments in more than 70 languages are among the 6,000 styles of ornaments available.

- Each year Bronner's guests purchase more than 1.3 million ornaments, over 700,000 feet of garland, nearly 100,000 postcards, and over 135,000 light sets (approximately 530 miles of light cords).

- More than 350 decorated trees and more than 700 animated figurines are displayed in Bronner's salesroom.

- Each decorated tree at Bronner's includes a Nativity ornament.

COLLECTIBLES

- Bronner's Hummel collection has over 1,000 figurines, one of most every subject produced for purchase.

- Bronner's annual M.I. Hummel Days event originated in 1980. Bronner's annual Precious Moments Days event began in 1983.

- Bronner's collection of Precious Moments figurines totals over 1,700, one of most every subject produced for purchase in the collection's first 25 years.

- More than 500 Nativities from 70 nations are part of Bronner's collection on display in the program center.

VISITOR INFORMATION

- Over two million guests visit annually from throughout the world.

- The weekend after Thanksgiving is Bronner's busiest of the year with about 50,000 guests.

- Each year 2,000 motorcoach groups visit Bronner's.

- Over a million guests have viewed the "World of Bronner's."

AWARDS & HONORS

- Goebel honored Bronner's as its 1997 National Retailer of the Year.
- Bronner's was the first recipient of the international Golden Santa Claus award in 1986, presented in Nuremberg, Germany.
- Bronner's was the first recipient of the NOEL (National Ornaments and Electric Lights Christmas Association) Retailer of the Year award in New York in 1981 and received the award again in 2001.
- The Automobile Club of Michigan (AAA) listed Bronner's among the top 10 man-made attractions in the state. AAA-Chicago Motor Club listed Bronner's as a "Travel Treasure."
- The governor of Michigan designated Bronner's as an "Embassy for Michigan Tourism" in 1976.
- In addition, Bronner's has received over 100 national, state, and regional awards. The Bronner family feels that every award focuses on the Bronner team members who helped make the recognition possible.

OTHER INTERESTING FACTS

- In peak season, Bronner's employs over 500 staff members.
- Movie star John Wayne ordered a Santa suit from Bronner's by telephone on December 15, 1976.
- Bronner's has more than 60 billboards - the most distant is on I-75 near Ocala, Florida, north of Disney World.
- Annually, Bronner's distributes over 1 million Christian tracts - one is inserted in each package and piece of mail leaving Bronner's.

Biographical Information

Wallace "Wally" Bronner, Frankenmuth, Michigan

CHURCH RECORD:

- Member of St. Lorenz Lutheran Church, served as deacon.

- Frequent speaker at church conventions, conferences and seminars, including Keynote Speaker for Lutheran Church Synodical Fiscal Conferences and Michigan Stewardship Conference.

- Member of Gideons International.

- Past chairman of Church Council, School Building and Church Building Fund Drives, Evangelism Committee, and Board of Elders.

- Former president and executive board member of Wheat Ridge Foundation, World Missions for Lutheran Church - Missouri Synod, and Camp Arcadia Association. Former member of Michigan District's Youth Committee and Board of Parish Education.

2002
- Christus Vivit Award by Concordia Seminary, St. Louis.

1992-93
- Honorary co-chair, with wife Irene, of the Franken Colonies Mission Fund (FCMF) for The Oswald Hoffmann School of Christian Outreach, Concordia College, St. Louis, Missouri.

- Member of planning committee for the 1993 reunion gathering celebrating the 100th Anniversary of the founding of the International Walther League.

1986
- Recipient of Miles Christi (Soldier of Christ) award by Concordia Theological Seminary, Ft. Wayne, Indiana.

- Walther League International president, 1958-1961.

BUSINESS RECORD:

- Originator, chairman of the board, and active in the daily business of BRONNER'S CHRISTmas WONDERLAND in Frankenmuth, Michigan. Bronner's features the world's largest year-round display of indoor and outdoor Christmas decorations; employs 500 full-time and part-time in the creation, design, distribution and importation of decorations from around the world; and distributes to over 1,000 retailers nationwide.

- Originator and former president and board chairman of Bronner Screen Printing, Inc. and Memtron Technologies. (Business sold to Donald and Karen Fischer, October 1984.)

- While visiting Oberndorf, Austria's, Silent Night Chapel during the early 1970's, Wally was inspired with the idea of duplicating that chapel in Frankenmuth. Formal permission was granted by the City and Visitors' Bureau of Oberndorf near Salzburg in November 1989. Three years later, Bronner's Silent Night Memorial Chapel replica was dedicated. The chapel was erected in thankfulness to God and as a tribute to the Christmas hymn "Silent Night" from the Wally and Irene Bronner family. One verse of "Silent Night" in over 300 languages and the message of Christ's Birth, Luke 2:l-19, in various languages is on display.

- Bronner's proclaimed a Michigan Embassy of Tourism by the governor of Michigan. Over 2 million annual visitors to Bronner's in Frankenmuth.
- Member of Circle Michigan Tourist Association.
- Recognized as a major attraction by AAA (American Automobile Association), CAA (Canadian Automobile Association), and DAA (Dominion Automobile Association).
- Frequent subject of regional, national and international television and radio programs, magazine and trade periodicals, and newspapers.
- Board President of Wallace & Irene Bronner Family Charitable Foundation.

2005
- Bronner's named Michigan Retailer of the Year.

2003
- Selected Retailer Award GCA (Garden Centers of America) Holiday Garden Center Tour.
- Silver ADDY Award presented by the Advertising Federation of the Saginaw Valley for production of the video "A Decorative Life: The Wally Bronner Story."

2001
- First-ever Impact in Ministry Award by Inspirational Giftware Magazine and Strang Communications at first IGGY (Inspirational Giftware Gift of the Year) Awards program.
- First-ever "Retailer of the Year" award in 1981 & repeat award in 2001 presented by the NOEL Association.
- Goebel 1997 National Retailer of the Year Award.

1995
- 50th Year BRONNER'S CHRISTmas WONDERLAND.

1994
- Hall of Fame Award by NOEL Association.

1990
- Named honored member of WHO's WHO in U.S. Executives.

1986
- Awarded first-ever, worldwide "Golden Santa" (for creativity and new ideas) at the Nuremberg Trade Fair.

CIVIC RECORD:

- Chamber of Commerce: Frankenmuth, State of Michigan, and the United States.
- Blue Cross/Blue Shield Customer Advisory Council.
- Frankenmuth Beautification Committee.
- Frankenmuth Lions Club.
- Frequent motivational speaker, master of ceremonies, song leader & keynote speaker at Saginaw Valley University entrepreneurship forums and seminars.
- Master Entrepreneur Award, Saginaw Valley University.
- Anglo-Celtic Society of Nativitists.
- Former board member of First of America Bank, Independent Business Association, Michigan State Chamber of Commerce, Greater Frankenmuth Corp., Frankenmuth Development Corp., Alma College Parent Advisory, & International Professional Display Association.

2005

- U.S. Postal Service "Potter Award" for most improved company by postal standards; presented by U.S. Postmaster General Jack Potter.

2004

- Robert H. Albert Community Service Award, Saginaw County Chamber of Commerce.
- NMA (National Management Association) Hall of Fame Award sponsored by BCBSM Management Association.

2003

- First-ever Outstanding Achievement in Michigan Tourism award by Travel Michigan.
- Pinnacle Award, Saginaw County Convention & Visitors Bureau.
- Lifetime honorary members, Frankenmuth Chamber of Commerce (Wally & Irene).
- Distinguished Alumni Award, Davenport University.
- Friend of Youth Award, Frankenmuth School District (Wally & Irene and Family).

2002

- Inaugural recipient, Wallace J. Bronner Excellence in Business Award, Davenport University.
- Mid-Michigan Distinguished Philanthropist Award (Wally & Irene).

2001

- Sons of the American Revolution Silver Good Citizenship Medal and Certificate of Commendation for Exemplary Patriotism awards.

2000

- MDA (Muscular Dystrophy Association) first-ever Spirit of Sharing award (Wally and Irene).
- Vision of Free Enterprise Award, Saginaw County Chamber of Commerce.

1999

- Co-Chair with wife Irene, Centennial Campaign of Lutheran Child & Family Service of Michigan.
- Laureate for Junior Achievement of Northeast Michigan.
- Silver Medallion of Honor for Research, Culture, & Religion presented by governor of the State of Salzburg, Austria, at Joseph Mohr Symposium, for helping inform the world about the origin and significance of "Silent Night."

1998

- Christmas Seals honorary chairman, American Lung Association of Michigan.

- Honorary Doctorate of Letters degree, Davenport University (formerly Great Lakes College).
- Honorary chairman Holiday Greeting Card Campaign, American Cancer Society of Michigan (also 1997 & 1996).

1997
- National Blue Chip Enterprise Initiative Award.
- All Area Arts Award, Saginaw Community Enrichment Commission.
- Friend of the Friendless Award, Saginaw Rescue Mission.
- Honorary chairman, Saginaw County U.S. Marine Corps Reserve Toys for Tots ('98 & '97).

1996
- "Frank N. Andersen Spirit of Philanthropy" award, Saginaw Community Foundation.

1995
- Michigan delegate, White House Conference on Tourism & member of Tourism Task Force.
- Michigan Master Entrepreneur of the Year.
- Honorary Rotarian.

1993
- Spring Arbor College Dedicated Service Award.
- Saginaw Community Foundation Trustee.
- Frankenmuth Lions Club named Wally a Lions Club International Foundation "Melvin Jones Fellow" for dedicated humanitarian services.
- Honorary National Girl Scout, Michigan's Mitten Bay Council.

1992
- Honorary chair Saginaw Rescue Mission Community Village Project.
- Member of Austria's Silent Night Association.

1991
- Outstanding Alumni Award, Davenport University (formerly Great Lakes College).

1989
- Rotary International "Paul Harris Fellowship" by Frankenmuth Rotary Club (Wally & Irene).

1988
- Frankenmuth Jaycees Herbert L. Keinath Distinguished Award.
- Salvation Army Others Award and Co-chair with wife Irene for State of Michigan annual Christmas Kettle Drive.

1987
- Member of Governor James J. Blanchard's Task Force on Future of Tourism.

1983
- Arthur Hill High School honor alumnus.

1979
- Served on executive council for Michigan Conference on Small Business and delegate to the White House Conference on Small Business.

FAMILY RECORD:

- Born: March 9, 1927
- Residence: Frankenmuth, Michigan 48734
- Married: Irene Pretzer on June 23, 1951
- Irene is member of Board of Directors and active in the business.
- Four Children: Wayne, Carla, Randall, and Maria.
- Wayne is President and CEO of the corporation. Wayne's wife Lorene is on Bronner's management team. Wayne and Lorene have two sons, Dietrich and Garrett.
- Carla is vice president. Carla's husband Bob is on Bronner's management team.
  Carla and Bob have three sons, Ryan, Paul, and Greg.
- Maria is vice president. Maria's husband Chris is on Bronner's management team.
- Randy lives in Arizona.

Videos ◆ DVDs ◆ Books
about BRONNER'S CHRISTmas WONDERLAND

VIDEOS & DVDS

"Christmas Dreams Come True" The story of BRONNER'S CHRISTmas WONDERLAND

        15-minute Video   #1021-397   15-minute DVD   #1083-604

"A Decorative Life" The Wally Bronner Story

        26-minute Video   #1078-027

"Silent Night Holy Night" narrated by Wally Bronner

        The story of the world's favorite carol, the composers, the memorial chapel in Oberndorf/Salzburg Austria and the authorized chapel replica in Frankenmuth, Michigan.

        25-minute Video   #1062-880

"Silent Night...A song around the World"

        Produced by Tepefilm - Features singing in English and 12 additional languages. Christmas greetings in various languages narrated by Wally Bronner.

        25-minute Video   #1005-817

"Decorator Collection" Themed Christmas Trees

        Produced by Verdoni Productions

        30-minute Video   #1089-077

BOOKS

"Picturesque story of BRONNER'S CHRISTmas WONDERLAND"

        as related by Wally Bronner

        254 pages #1108-800

"BRONNER'S" Souvenir Colorful Photo Book (11" x 8.5")

        24 pages   #1062-793

"Ornament Legends, Symbols & Traditions"

        40 pages   #1095-844

Ordering information visit www.bronners.com

FUTURE RELEASES:

"Sharing JOY 365 Days a Year"

        Autobiography of Wally Bronner

"111 Reflections...plus" by Wally Bronner

        111 Quips, 111 phrases, 111 reflections, 111 speech excerpts and 111 awards.

"CHRISTmas Commentary and Wonders" by Wally Bronner

        Sharing the spirit of CHRISTmas via experiences and traditions.

APPENDIX